John Bryan

Fables and essay

Volume I.

John Bryan

Fables and essay
Volume I.

ISBN/EAN: 9783744768955

Printed in Europe, USA, Canada, Australia, Japan

Cover: Foto ©ninafisch / pixelio.de

More available books at **www.hansebooks.com**

FABLES AND ESSAYS

BY

JOHN BRYAN

OF OHIO

VOL. I.

[*COMPLETE IN ITSELF*]

FIFTH THOUSAND.

NEW YORK
THE ARTS AND LETTRES CO.
1895

COPYRIGHT, 1895, BY JOHN BRYAN

[*All rights reserved*]

72043

Press of J. J. Little & Co.
Astor Place, New York

AUTHOR'S NOTE.

This book is dedicated to two ideas which are equally inclusive: *Liberty, Justice.*

This book is copyrighted to prevent others from selling it at a gainful price.

The words "Vol. I." were inserted in the title-page because, while this book was going to press, the author produced a number of other Fables, which will contribute to a future volume, whether the public like this volume or not.

The author would be pleased to receive any sincere approval or disapproval, in writing, from the readers of this book, addressed in care of the publishers.

PREFACE.

I suppose most authors publish their books for about the same reason a hen lays eggs—for relief to themselves. Under the circumstances the most amiable thing I can do is to humbly beg the public's pardon for perpetrating another book upon it. As it is not intended to be sold for profit I can not even plead as an excuse that it is expected to fill a long felt want. Besides I should be much obliged to the public for reading it at all, let alone pay a profit on its manufacture.

What if Jesus had copyrighted and charged a fee for his Sermon on the Mount?

One who gathers and writes news is worthy of hire: but what shall we say of the author who button-holes the impatient public upon the street and harangues it, and then, hat in hand, begs the strolling buffoon's fee?

Mr., Mrs., or Miss Reader, I respect you; and I assure you if I could see you coming out of a bookstore with my book under your arm I should almost feel that you were my friend. At least I should feel that after you read it you would know something of me, but I nothing of you, which would be friendship half seas over, for I do hope you will like such part of me as you find herein.

I expect you will pardon me, for you know as well as I there are emergencies in nature which a person can't help: there are times when a thing can no longer be concealed, and publication is a relief.

I've had these manuscripts about me for years and tried to suppress them untill those who knew me gave me a character of mystery and whispered among themselves that they expected something unusual from me: I've even "sat on the safety-valve" until I knew the explosion could no longer be delayed.

I even got my hair cut quite short and ordered fashionable clothes: but all to no purpose. So here I am, again begging your pardon, and thanking you in advance for granting it. If you read my book at all I shall feel that I have not exploded in vain.

THE AUTHOR.

For additional Preface see page 119.

CONTENTS.

	PAGE
AUTHOR'S NOTE,	iii
PREFACE,	v
THE DONKEY AND HIS MASTER,	5
THE BOY AND THE DOG,	7
THE HORSE AND THE ELK,	9
THE LION AND THE PEASANT,	12
THE LILY AND THE HOLLYHOCK,	14
THE MUSK-RAT AND THE HUNTER,	16
THE GRAY SQUIRREL AND THE POLITICIANS,	18
THE MAID AND THE FOWLS,	21
THE ANT GIVES A RECEPTION,	22
THE CARRION-DOG AND THE MASTIFF,	24
THE GOD AND THE DEVIL,	27
DOGS FIGHTING OVER A BONE,	33
THE FOX AND THE GEESE,	34
REWARD OF THE GODS,	39
THE FARMER, THE SHE-FOX, AND THE WOLF,	43
THE HORSE IN CLOVER,	45
THE BEGGING MONK,	49
THE CATS AND THE SPARROWS,	52
AND THIS IS LOVE,	55

	PAGE
THE DOG AND HIS MUTTON,	57
THE HUNTER AND THE RABBIT,	60
THE RAT AND THE RABBITS,	62
THE JUST GOVERNOR,	73
THE MAN AND THE FLY,	74
THE LUXURIOUS CATS,	75
THE PULLET AND THE CHICKS,	77
THE GENIE AND THE VALLEY,	79
THE WAITING BUZZARDS,	86
THE DEVIL, THE GOD, AND THE MAN,	87
THE DOGS AND THE PEASANT,	89
THE CUNNING THIEF,	91
EXPERIENCE AGAINST TEARS,	92
THE SHEEP AND THE SHEPHERD,	93
EVERY TREE LEANS,	94
THE POISONED RATS,	95
THE CONCEITED DONKEY,	97
THE BREACHY COW,	100
THE COWS AND THE BULLS,	102
FATE'S TRUE LOVE,	106
SUPPLEMENTARY PREFACE,	119
BOY-TALK,	121
THE YOUNG ROBINS,	125
THE PUPPY AND EXPERIENCE,	132
A MAN AND HIS TROWSERS,	134
THE WOMEN WHO SAW A GOD,	135
THE FOX AND THE WOOD-DUCK,	140
DO THEY REMEMBER?	146

	PAGE
NEVER A DREAM,	147
MY HARP AND I,	148
THERE WAS LOVE IN HER EYES,	151
THE HEART OF MY SWEETHEART,	153
THE LOVER'S LAY,	155
TO ...., ON HER FIFTEENTH BIRTHDAY,	157
LISTENING LOVE,	158
TO .... "LIKE A HARP,"	161
NEW YEAR'S GREETING,	162
MATING-DAY,	163
TO A YOUNG LADY,	164
YOU TOUCHED ME,	165
THOU ART MY SEA,	167
TO A LADY,	168
ON SEEING A REPTILE,	169
TO A WOMAN,	171
JOHN GANDY AND I,	172
THE HAWK, THE CROW, AND THE HEN,	177
THE PRIEST AND THE SAGE,	178
TRANQUILLITY,	180
ABOUT WOMAN,	183
ABOUT MOTHERHOOD,	187
DO NOT SELL,	191
FIGHTING FOR A POTATO-PATCH,	192
THE VAIN GARDENER,	193
THE WIFE OF A WOLF,	195
THE CONSPIRING ANIMALS,	196
JUPITER AND THE BIRDS,	200

	PAGE
ABOUT MARRIAGE, ... 203	
JUPITER AND THE ANTS, ... 211	
THE HEIFER AND THE ROSES, ... 212	
THE OX WITH THE SILVER FLANKS, . . . 214	
IN A CERTAIN COUNTRY, ... 218	
THE AUTHOR AND THE READER, ... 221	
THE TREES AND THE GARDENERS, . . 224	
ABOUT THE FABLE, ... 228	
THE NEWSPAPER—THE THEATRE, . . . 231	
TWO LETTERS TO ELZA, ... 234	
TELL ME, ... 244	
I'M TIRED, ... 245	

THE DONKEY AND HIS MASTER.

A donkey who was employed by his master to carry upon his back great sacks of oats, stopped suddenly one day upon the highway.

"Go on, thou beast," said the man.

"I can go no farther," brayed the donkey.

"Thou ungrateful beast," said the man, "do I not give thee work by which thou dost earn thy feed?"

"Alas," said the donkey, "my burdens are so heavy and my feed so light that I am too weak to trudge farther."

"If thou dost not go on I shall lose the

market for my grain. Go on, or I will goad thee!" said the man.

The donkey still refused to proceed, whereupon the man began to goad him severely. The donkey resented this by kicking and shaking every sack of grain from his back to the ground, which so frightened the man that he called to a passerby for help.

There was a kind look in the stranger's eyes as he said to the man:

"Thou art rightly served; the donkey can carry the whole load if thou puttest less of it on his back and more of it in his stomach."

MORAL:

The solution of the problem between the employer and the employed.

THE BOY AND THE DOG.

A half-grown boy was promised a large piece of bread and butter, with sugar and jelly on it, if he would perform a certain laborious task.

Having well performed the task he went out on the steps to eat his bread and butter. He sat with his elbows on his knees and began to eat with characteristic voracity, when a dog came and sat before him and looked with such evident hunger and longing that the boy turned himself to the left to avoid the pleadings of the dog.

But the dog again placed himself in

front of the boy with some propitiating wags of his tail and a still more begging look. The boy now turned himself squarely to the right, the bread and butter almost sticking in his throat. Again the dog took a position in front of the boy. Saliva was dripping from the dog's jaws, and he almost leaped toward the boy, so great was his evident expectation and desire.

"Damn that dog!" said the boy as he went into the house to eat his bread and butter.

MORAL:

One who is sympathetic can not enjoy, in the presence of the poor, what he himself has honestly earned.

THE HORSE AND THE ELK.

An Elk who was browsing upon the scant, dry twigs of the winter forest, was accosted by a horse who peered over the fence of a neighboring field:

"You look hungry, my friend," said the Horse.

"I am both hungry and lonesome," said the Elk.

"It is about what you deserve," said the Horse; "why don't you come over into the fields and become civilized?"

"I prefer the innocence and freedom of the forest," said the Elk.

"If you joined our society and submitted to our rules," said the Horse, "you would be fit to be associated with. I am really ashamed to be seen talking with you."

"You addressed me first," said the Elk, "and since you opened the conversation, I will tell you a bit of news. Over by the edge of the forest yonder I saw two men coming this way with a halter and straps and chains. I heard by their conversation that one had just bargained with the other for the sale of a horse."

"Alas!" said the Horse, "I know not who will be my master or where my home shall be."

"I may be uncivilized, but nobody owns me," said the Elk as he bounded away through the forest.

MORAL:

Liberty is preferable to all things else.

THE LION AND THE PEASANT.

A Lion once fell in love with the daughter of a Peasant. When he desired to visit her the Peasant, who had recently lost his valuable watch-dog, consented to his visits on condition that the Lion should protect the house from some robbers who lived in a mountain near by.

In pursuance of this arrangement, the Lion was often about the house, where he behaved with subdued and becoming manners owing to his great affection for the daughter.

The Peasant soon grew familiar with the Lion and ordered him to keep at a distance from the house, saying that when he needed his protection he would call him.

The Lion started away, but when he was near the edge of the forest the peasant called to him with great earnestness to come back, as the robbers were attacking the house.

"Make your own defense," said the Lion; "I am not a dog that I can be scolded away and whistled back again."

THE LILY AND THE HOLLY-HOCK.

"Why do you keep nodding to every passerby?" said a Holly-hock to a Lily.

"The wind bends me," said the Lily; "but really I think my nodding as becoming as your stiff, haughty manner."

"My stalk is so rigid I can not bend," said the Holly-hock, "but I wouldn't nod at everybody as you do if I could."

The gardener, who was passing by, said to his son: "I think the frost to-night will cut down all our lilies and holly-hocks."

MORAL:

We should neither be vain of our own nor envy the natural qualities of others; for nature gave them and she will soon take them away.

The Musk-Rat and The Hunter.

A Musk-Rat, to escape the Hunter, took refuge in a deep hole which he had dug in the bank of a pond. When the Hunter began to dig at the entrance of the hole, the Musk-Rat came forward near enough to be heard and said to the Hunter:

"Why do you dig at the entrance of my house?"

"I want to get you, Mr. Musk-Rat," said the Hunter.

"What do you want of me?" said the Musk-Rat.

"I want your skin," said the man,

"and if you will only come out you will save me a great deal of trouble in digging you out."

"My skin is worth more to me than it is to you," said the Musk-Rat, "and if you get it you will have to dig for it, and dig faster at this end of my hole than I do at the other end."

"The sly devil," said the man to his son, "let us go home; his skin is not worth the labor."

MORAL:

1. Do not facilitate the efforts of those who seek to injure you.

2. Resist your enemies to the last, and they will often abandon their attack disheartened.

3. The wit of the weak often defeats the determination of the strong.

The Gray Squirrel
and the Politicians.

Two politicians of different parties went into a forest to hunt squirrels. Having treed a squirrel, one of them stood on one side of the tree and one on the other. One of them at last drew aim at the squirrel, when the latter cried out:

"What are you—Republican or Democrat?"

"Republican," said the man; "what is that to you?"

"It is a good deal to me, sir," said the Squirrel; "if you were a Democrat you might shoot all day at me, for they never hit a mark they aim at."

"That Squirrel is too smart to be killed," said the man, lowering his gun.

By this time the other man took aim, when the Squirrel called out:

"Democrat or Republican?"

"Democrat," said the man.

"Then you had better shoot at that black squirrel in the other tree yonder."

As the Democrat turned his head to look for the black squirrel, the gray squirrel crept down the trunk of the tree into a hole and was safe.

"Hello!" cried the two men, at once standing together: "Come out, Mr. Squirrel, and we shall be friends. We won't shoot."

"Honor bright?" barked the Squirrel from behind the side of the hole.

"Honor bright," said the men.

At this the Squirrel came to the door of the hole.

"Why did you ask our politics?" said the men.

"I did it," said the Squirrel, "to gain time to escape. My old father used to say that he could tell a Democrat 'by the way he shot;' but you can't do it now. As you are both politicians I can't trust either of you. Good-day, gentlemen."

MORAL:

Between the two parties the people have a hard time.

THE MAID AND THE FOWLS.

A young cock, who had been brought but recently into the farm-yard, asked an older cock why it was that when the Farmer, who was master of all the lands, came to his door the fowls were indifferent toward him or ran away in fear; but when the Maid came to the door they ran to her in great numbers.

"She often comes to the door to shake the table-cloth," said the older cock.

MORAL:

1. Generous persons will have many friends.

2. We often get credit for generosity when we do not deserve it.

THE ANT GIVES A RECEPTION.

An ant whose parents had been very poor married a male who by his shrewdness had accumulated great stores. She set great merit upon herself for this reason, and amid her plenty, determined to give a reception to all the other ants.

She with several others, stood up in a row and invited the rest to pass along before her and make a sign of honor to her.

While this reception was in progress a great shadowy object came moving along the road, making so much dust and noise that most of the company were wont to run away.

"Stay," said the ant, "it is only an elephant who is coming to my reception."

MORAL:

The conceit of those who give receptions is unbounded.

The Carrion-Dog and the Mastiff.

A dog who was very fond of carrion met a respectable Mastiff who was standing in the open gate of his Master's yard.

"Hello, Mastiff," said the Carrion-dog, "I've just struck the scent of a royal bit of carrion. Don't you smell it? Come, let's follow it up."

"No; I don't smell it, and I wouldn't follow it up if I did," said the Mastiff.

"Whiff — whiff," sniffed the Carrion-dog, "that's a glorious breeze; I can follow it straight as a bee line. I promise you the tid-bits. Besides if there are any common curs who have already scented it, they will be frightened away by your massive strength."

"I will not go along with you, sir; also, I would thank you to not stand so close to me; your breath is very bad, and I have been taught to avoid those whose breath smells of what they eat and drink."

About this time the dog-catcher, who was passing by, threw his net over the Carrion-dog and dragged him yelping and struggling away. The Mastiff remained standing at the gate until the dog-catcher was quite out of sight, then he turned and walked slowly to meet his kind Master who came down the steps.

"I have seen and heard it all," said the Master, patting the Mastiff on the head. "Remember this

MORAL:

Justice is often upon the heels of the wicked while they ply their nefarious ways."

Or, "Every one to his taste and also to his fate."

THE GOD AND THE DEVIL.

A god and a devil met each other while they were traveling through space and began to dispute as to their comparative strength and powers. They soon decided to alight upon some planet of the universe and put themselves to comparative tests to settle the dispute.

Just at that moment the clouds of earth seemed to separate and revealed that part of the earth's surface called America. With one accord they sped through the opening and chose the United States as their field.

Both being immortal, years or centuries of time were but as moments.

Each tried his strength upon the earth. One quaked the earth at New Madrid, the other at Charleston. They tried their strength upon the winds; one destroyed Grinnell,* the other whirled Pomeroy† into ruins.

Unable to decide, they held a conference and agreed to test their powers upon human beings themselves. They began to respect each other as worthy opponents, and really became friends.

The devil spoke first, saying he had heard from time immemorial that his ancestor had beguiled the first woman—the mother of all living, by assuming the disguise of a serpent.

So they separated, each agreeing to re-

*Grinnell, Iowa, Tornado, June, 17, 1882.
†Pomeroy, Iowa, Tornado, July 6, 1893.

port at their next meeting his success or failure in attempting to beguile a woman.

The devil saw a woman walking in a garden. He assumed the form of a serpent and appeared before her with friendly blandishments. But she fled from him with terror. He threw himself before her whichever way she fled. She turned each time with dismay and was almost given up to despair when he suddenly changed himself into a Priest, who seemed to be hunting the serpent to slay it. The woman hastened to the priest, gave her money to him, threw herself into his arms and yielded up her will to him. When night had come he left her sleeping. When morning awoke her, her eyes were dazzled by the light, her hair was disheveled, and there was a stain upon her garment.

"O, God," said she, "how horrible was my dream." And when she saw the stain upon her garment, she bowed her face into her hands and wept.

The god saw a woman in her bath, and he took the invisible form of her own thoughts. He whispered to her; "Thou art beautiful; thou shouldst have a lover."

And when she was walking in a garden in the after part of the day he appeared before her as a beautiful youth, like unto Apollo, who sat under a bower reading a book. And when he heard the rustle of her garments he affected to be startled, and would have moved away had she not spoken and held him by her beauty. She blushed and said:

"Sir, what book do you read?"

He bowed low and handed it to her upon the fold of his silken robe. And she saw it was "The Book of Love." She returned it to him, and by her pleased looks he knew she wished him to read it to her. They sat down and each held a side of the book, and as he read, his voice was sweet and tender; and after a while there were tears in her eyes, and she looked down lest he should see them. When evening was come he touched her hand and she did not draw it back.

He arose and walked away, and she followed him as if in a dream farther and farther into the shades of the night and of the garden.

When morning awoke her, her eyes were dazzled by the light, her hair was disheveled and there was a stain upon her garment.

"O, God," said she, "how beautiful was my dream." And when she saw the stain upon her garment, her face was tranquil and happy, for she knew she had been touched by a god.

MORAL:

Shall the God of Love or the Priests of Religion decide the destiny of Woman.

DOGS FIGHTING OVER A BONE.

Two dogs were fighting over a bone which lay on the ground between them.

"While the dogs are occupied in fighting," whispered a pebble to the bone, "is your opportunity to run away."

"Not so," said the bone, "for if I run away they will have no longer cause for combat, and one of them will pursue me and gnaw me quite up. So long as they continue to fight I am safe."

MORAL:

The conflict of the Catholics and the Protestants over the Public Schools.

THE FOX AND THE GEESE.

A Fox once fell in love with a fat young goose who was the pride of her family. He desired to marry her, calculating that in many ways the alliance would be to his advantage; for he knew she would be a fat, tender wife, besides he expected it would give him ample opportunities to carry on many sly depredations among the rest of her flock.

So one day he approached old Mr. Gander, the father of young Miss Goose, and after several low bows and gracious smiles, he proposed for her in marriage.

Old Mr. Gander wisely concealed his

astonishment that this well-known enemy of his race should propose for his daughter; for he quickly suspected it foreboded a scheme of making her and many of the flock the prey of Mr. Fox.

"Have you spoken to my daughter, sir?" said old Mr. Gander with as much dignity as he could command.

"I have not spoken to her," said Mr. Fox, "but I have long admired her, and my ancestors have always had a liking for geese, sir."

"I remember well, sir," said old Mr. Gander, "your noble grandfather came from across the pond and took a cousin of mine to be his wife abroad; but once we heard of her being unmercifully plucked, and after that we have not learned what became of her. Do you wish to take my daughter abroad with you, sir?"

"On the contrary," said Mr. Fox, "I expect to be so gentle and gracious that you will accept me among your own household."

"I will speak to my daughter and her mother concerning the matter this evening, and report our decision to-morrow," said old Mr. Gander. "Good-day, Mr. Fox."

"Good-day, Mr. Gander," said Mr. Fox, as he turned and trotted toward the forest.

The next day Mr. Fox met old Mr. Gander in the pasture, and was told that if he would call at the great Goose House that evening, he would be introduced to

Miss Goose, and receive such a reception as one of his rank and kind deserved. "My daughter has long admired your beautiful brush," said old Mr. Gander, "and I have no doubt that if you behave becomingly, this will be her wedding night,"

Mr. Fox was greatly pleased and promised to be on hand at the proper hour.

It was arranged that Miss Goose should be married that very evening to young Mr. Gander, and that the ceremony should be spoken in goose language, which Mr. Fox could not understand. So he sat up prim, and vainly smiled and coiled his brush around in front of him, and looked on with apparent great interest.

When the ceremony was complete, and it was explained to Mr. Fox what had happened, he became greatly enraged and declared that he would make a meal of her anyhow; whereupon the several ganders flew upon him and the geese set up such a cackling that the farmer came running with his dogs to see what was the matter, and catching Mr. Fox, as he thought, in the midst of his depredations, dispatched him instantly.

MORALS:

1. Sometimes by experience geese become as wise as foxes.

2. How unwise in Mr. Fox to not know that the object of his attentions to a goose would be suspected; and

3. How foolish in him to expect that a goose would marry any one but a gander.

4. The wisest are sometimes foolish in love.

REWARD OF THE GODS.

A being, whom it was decreed Jupiter should send upon the earth, was given its choice as to what form of animal it should be embodied in. In order to form an intelligent decision, the being asked of Jupiter such knowledge as the gods only possess, as to the state, degree, and characteristics of the various forms of animal life upon the earth. Jupiter suggested that it might have the choice of becoming a man or a jack-ass. "If you become a man," continued Jupiter, "you will have to be born of woman; if you become a jack-ass, you will have to be born of a gennette."

"Permit me," said the being, "to see the woman and the gennette so that I may make choice of a mother."

Jupiter rolled the clouds of earth back, so as to make one small window through which the being peered. It saw a woman in her bath, who was as beautiful as Venus, and a gennette upon the street with two huge baskets of fruit strapped upon her sides, and a skin filled with water upon her crup.

"Before I choose," said the being, "I beg one other privilege: permit me to see a man and a jack-ass."

Jupiter rolled the clouds away again.

The being looked and saw a man who was the lover of the woman; the muscles of his sides were bands of strength, his thighs were like pillars, and his passion was like a god's; but his eyes were full of tenderness.

The being also saw a jack-ass on a village common. On his back were several rollicking children, and some clung to his tail; others tugged at his halter, and still others worried his ears as he ambled along.

"I will be a jack-ass," said the being.

"So mote it be," said Jupiter.

After 30 years, the length of life of the jack-ass, the being, having completed the decree of fate, returned to Jupiter.

"By what reason," inquired Jupiter, "didst thou choose thy condition upon earth?"

"I saw in the eyes of the gennette and of the jack-ass," said the being, "humility, patience and forbearance; besides one being if not another must be be a jackass on earth, and I had as good a right to be it as any."

"Thy wisdom and thy charity are equal to a god's," said Jupiter; "henceforth thou shalt be a god."

MORAL:

The god's reward men for making jackasses of themselves.

THE FARMER, THE SHE-FOX AND THE WOLF.

A poor and hungry, but honest she-fox once went boldly to a farmer's house, and knocking at the door told the farmer frankly of her great want, and the sore distress of her young at home in the forest.

The weather being bleak and cold, the farmer commended the fox's honesty and compassionately gave her a supply of food for herself and young.

The fox came daily and carried away a goodly supply of food; but after many days the farmer observed that she remained as lean and hungry as ever.

"Take your gun," said the farmer to his son, "and watch the path of the fox, and see if you can solve this mystery."

When the son returned he said to the farmer:

"I expect the she-fox and her young will now get fat, for I have shot and killed the fat wolf who daily waylaid and robbed her."

MORAL:

1. The honest poor are often made so by the shrewdness and oppression of others.

2. See that what thou givest to the poor does not go to fatten some rascal who robs them of that thou givest them.

THE HORSE IN CLOVER.

A horse stood in the middle of a field up to his knees and up to his eyes in clover.

His form was round and shapely, and his coat glossy and sleek, his tail and mane flowing and full, his hoofs hard and round, his ear quick and versatile, his eyes bright and intelligent, his nostril dilated and sensitive, his lip firm, his teeth white and young.

He brushed the bees from the nodding clover blossoms, and plucked the sweetest of them at his leisure here and there. It was a day in June, and the sun was shining and the murmur of a brook could be heard amid some leafy trees near by.

"How happy am I," said the horse, "I toil not and I want not."

With these words he began to look around him and question why his life was happy within and plenteous without; and which of these was the cause of the other.

When he looked around to enjoy the landscape, he saw on every side of his field great numbers of horses. Many of them were old and most of them overworked and all hungry and poor.

His first impulse was to throw down the fences and invite them all into his pasture.

- He was proceeding to carry this benevolent feeling into action when a call from his kind master stopped him.

"If you throw down the fences," said his master, "they will soon devour all this luxuriant clover up by the roots, and you will be as poor as they."

"But I can share my plenty with them," said the horse.

"Is it better," said the man, "that there should be 99 poor horses and one fat one, or 100 poor ones?"

"It is better that there should be but 99 poor horses," said the horse, "but how came they all to be so poor and I so plenteously provided for?"

"Their masters have robbed them, and if you gave to them of your plenty, their masters would rob them of that thou gavest them, and they would remain as poor as ever."

"Alas," said the horse, "I am unhappy."

MORAL:

Giving unto the poor enriches not them, but those who rob them.

THE BEGGING MONK.

A monk who belonged to a very wealthy order went forth to beg, pleading great poverty and distress to those from whom he asked alms. He met a butcher and a baker to whom he said he had eaten nothing for many days, and that he was almost starved.

"How is it thou art so fat?" said they as they drove on their wagons.

He met a tradesman and said he had not had any money for years, even from his youth, as he had long been a monk.

"I have no money to give thee," said the tradesman, at the same time jingling a handful of gold coins in his pocket.

"I pray Jesus to forgive thee that lie," said the monk, "for I hear the coins jingling in thy pockets."

"If thou hast seen so little money in thy life," said the tradesman, "how dost thou so well know its jingle?"

He met a fish-monger carrying a basket of fish, coming from attending his nets, to whom he said: "I and my brothers are perishing for want of fish. Pray give us thy basket of fish and go thou and catch others."

"Go and catch thy own fish," said the fish-monger, "the waters of the earth are as free for thee to fish in as for me."

He met a woman at her door to whom he bowed low and made the sign of the cross:

"Kind Madam," said he, "I and my

brothers are perishing for want of food and money; I pray you give unto us according as the Lord hath prospered thee."

"Come in, poor Monk," said she, "we have not much except my husband's wages, but to share with thee is to give unto the Lord."

So saying she gave him half her savings; and when he made ready to depart, she craved his blessing.

"You may kiss my signet ring or my great toe," said he. Which being done, he departed, and with a shrug of his shoulders, said to himself:

"Ah, if women were not so easily beguiled, we should be compelled to work or starve indeed."

MORAL:

Scrutinize closely those who ask charity.

THE CATS AND THE SPARROWS.

The cats and the sparrows once held a conference at which the cats proposed that if the sparrows would consent to roost low, they would protect them at night from their enemies. "For how can we climb to the topmost twigs to protect you," argued the cats.

"You have only recently claimed friendship for us yourselves," said the sparrows. "Give us some proof of your good faith."

"We will build you a small, strong house with a door only large enough for you to enter," said the cats; "and we will guard it from your enemies all the night."

To this fair proposal the sparrows agreed, and when the house was built, they came down in the evening and occupied it in great numbers. The cats invited many of their neighbors to help protect the door of the sparrows; and they faithfully kept their trust until morning.

When day dawned, the sparrows went to the door of their house and said: "We thank you, friends, for your faithful protection during the night; will you now kindly go away so that we may fly about our business?"

" No, thank you," said the cats: " we protected you from your enemies during the night with the expectation of ourselves having sparrows for breakfast this morning."

MORAL :

Do not trust to your own wit against the friendly proposals of a known enemy.

AND THIS IS LOVE.

A young man married a beautiful young girl whom he loved very much.

At their first meal he carved the steak, and out of his affection for her he gave her the tender part. This he continued to do without interruption, giving her the tender part of the steak at every meal for three years. On the morning of the third anniversary of their wedding he begged her to carve the steak—pleading as he pretended—that he had strained his wrist.

To this she readily consented, and as usual kept the tender part of the steak for herself.

The next morning, his wrist having suddenly recovered, he carved the steak himself, and kept the tender part for himself.

At this his wife burst into tears, exclaiming, " You no longer love me."

" Ah, Madam," said he, " I have done an act of selfishness only once which you have repeated a thousand times."

MORAL :

She applied for a divorce on the ground of extreme cruelty, and got it.

THE DOG AND HIS MUTTON.

One dark night a dog named Tray left his fellows in their kennels and went marauding among his master's sheep. He killed several and glutted himself with mutton.

Having satiated his appetite a sense of guilt and fear of detection on the morrow took possession of him. He began to work his wits to conceal his guilt. Having carefully removed the dirt of travel from his paws and the stain from his jaws, he stealthily returned to the kennel, careful to not wake his companions. As he had always carefully guarded his reputation he believed he would not be suspected and hoped the deed would be laid on some of the less stealthy dogs of the kennel, or on some innocent dog of the neighboring farms.

When the farmer learned in the early morning that his valuable sheep had been killed, he said to his sons: "We must determine whether the sheep-dog is among our own dogs before suspecting our neighbors."

So he bade his sons when they called all the dogs to give them their breakfast, to observe which dog had no appetite, for he expected the guilty one would not manifest his usual hunger.

But Tray being a shrewd villain, had expected this test would be made; and when the sons whistled the several dogs to breakfast, he ran as fast as he could with his full stomach and manifested even more hunger than usual. Then the sons said, "Surely Tray is not guilty, for we have not often seen him eat so heartily;" and they called the farmer to witness the fact of the evident innocence of every dog in their kennels.

The farmer was much gratified at this, but just as he was about to turn back into the house, Tray began to show signs of sickness, and began to vomit up not only his breakfast, but also the mutton he had eaten the night before.

"Who would have believed it," said the farmer with great sorrow. "Take the sheep-dog away and kill him."

MORAL:

Never try to conceal your foibles by violating the laws of nature.

THE HUNTER AND THE RABBIT.

—•o⟩⊙⟨o•—

The following fable was recited to me by a beautiful Syrian lady. It is probably the original of La Fontaine's "Satyr and the Hunter." It is so good, any one might wish to be the author of it.   J. B.

One cold day a man went hunting and he caught a rabbit which was so beautiful that he desired to keep her and take her to his home.

As they journeyed along the man blew his breath into his hands.

"Why do you do that?" asked the rabbit.

"To warm my hands," said the man.

At dinner the man seated the rabbit at the table with his children. As he ate his soup, which was very hot, she noticed he blew his breath upon it.

" Why do you blow your breath upon the broth ? " asked the rabbit.

" To cool it," said the man.

At this the rabbit leaped through the window and fled away saying :

" I am afraid to abide with one who can blow hot and cold with the same breath."

THE RAT AND THE RABBITS.

One day a low-born but aspiring rat met a rabbit in the way. "Hello," said the rat; "I have often heard my old father speak of what elegant people your family are, but I never had the honor of meeting one of you before." As he said this the rat made a low bow, and the rabbit sat up and put his ears forward and looked at the rat through his eye-glasses.

"I am no ordinary rat, sir," said the rat, "and I have often thought from what I had heard, that I resembled your kind, sir; and now that I have seen you, sir, I think better of the resemblance than ever."

At this the rat sat up and imitated the rabbit as well as he could, making himself look comical indeed.

The rabbit suppressed a smile, and assumed an interested air, as if to say: " By Jove, I'll have some fun." So walking around the rat and observing him critically, he said : " I really believe you would resemble our kind somewhat if it were not for that outrageous long, slim, round tail you drag behind you. Would you consent to have that cut off, sir ? "

" I would, sir, for the sake of getting into good society," said the rat, looking back at the file-like member, and glancing enviously at the rabbit's soft white one. " But," continued he, "don't you think I look as well with it as I would with no tail at all, sir? Besides, sir, if I have it cut off it will forever bar me from associating again with my own kind, sir."

" Never fear," said the rabbit, " we can stick on a bunch of cotton in its place, which will look quite like mine."

"Agreed," said the rat.

"All right," said the rabbit, "come with me to Surgeon Chip-Munk, and he will do the job for you in a jiffy."

Surgeon Chip-Munk sawed the tail off so close to the spinal column, that it made Mr. Rat have a weak back ever after. Having stuck a bunch of cotton on the wound, which was soon saturated with blood, he limped away with his new-found friend to join "good society" among the rabbits.

" Hello, Chappy," said one of Mr. Rabbit's friends, "what have you got there?"

"S-h-h," whispered Mr. Rabbit, "it's nothing but an ordinary rat who thought by cutting off his tail and sticking on a piece of cotton, he would resemble us rabbits. He wants to get into our set. Mr. Bunny, (aloud) allow me to introduce my friend, Mr. Cotton-tail." And so Mr. Rat took up his residence among the rabbits.

Mr. Rabbit and Mr. Bunny, as they went along with Cotton-tail limping behind, had a whispered agreement between themselves that they would let the chappies of their tribe know the true character of Cotton-tail, but they would intimate to the females of their several families that he was a titled foreigner; and when they suggested this to Cotton-tail, he readily assented, declaring that of a truth the bluest sort of blood ran in his veins, that his ancestors were originally from Norway, and that one of his very great grandfathers had come over in the Day-Flower.

(The fact is, as was well known among the rats of Rat Hollow, that this grandfather of his had to take refuge on the ship to escape a pack of terriers which the people had set after him on account of his outrageous stealing and other depredations. Also that he had been obliged to remain concealed in the steerage on the way over.)

"The blood in your tail was ordinary red," said Mr. Rabbit with a sly wink at Mr. Bunny. "However," he continued, "don't let that worry you, you'll pass for a regular blue-blooded foreign duke."

With this he slapped Cotton-tail on his

sore back, which made the poor devil limp up a little brighter, and he really began to consider what sort of a brogue he should adopt.

They introduced him to the females as the Duc de Cotton-tail, and the season of intense popularity he had among them almost turned his head, and he often wished the common rats in Rat Hollow could see him basking in their favors.

Several times his cotton-tail actually dropped off, exposing the scabby stump, but the females were too polite to notice it. Indeed, I half suspect some of the chappies occasionally jerked poor Cotton-tail's tail off for a joke, as they always seemed to have an uproar of fun covertly at his expense.

They often strided over him and nearly

stepped on him, offering the apology that they didn't see him. They called him the Runt of the Kid.

One day he went with the rabbits into the field to graze upon the fine grass, and you may believe he nearly starved trying to subsist on grass as the rabbits did. He became thin and weak, his coat was rough, his little round black eyes were scabby, his voice was squeaky, and his tail was plainly tied on with a string. The females, too, had begun to know his true character, and none of them would allow him near them. Indeed many a whisper and covert glance and suppressed giggle might have been seen as the troup of pleasure seekers gayly scampered toward the grazing grounds.

The chappies knew the party was liable

to be pursued by the dogs, and they had resolved to leave poor Cotton-tail to his fate. When the dogs came with yelp and clatter, the rabbits took to their heels and were soon away over the hills to a place of safety ; but poor Cotton-tail came limping and squealing after, and it was owing to his smallness that the dogs ran quite over him, though several snapped at him with horrid teeth. Amid a cloud of dust and a deal of fright and excitement he managed to crawl under the hollow root of an old stump, where, almost within reach of the dogs' claws and noses, he trembled and crouched in terror for hours until the dogs were finally called home by their master. He did not dare come out till next day, when he heard the rabbits come trooping back to graze again.

To their astonishment he presented himself among them alive, but the sorriest looking mortal it had ever been any one's fortune to see.

Out of pity the females urged the chappies to tell him he was well known to be only an ordinary low-born rat; that he would never be accepted in society, and that he would likely be killed. They recommended him to return to his kin in Rat Hollow.

To this he consented and to their credit they carried him on a litter (for rabbits are kind-hearted if weak-minded animals) to where upon the ill-fated day he first met Mr. Rabbit.

From this spot he made his way with great difficulty to Rat Hollow and presented himself to his kin. His father and mother had died during his absence. Rumors of his contemptible toadyism had spread throughout the neighborhood, and no one would consent to receive him, especially with that ridiculous stump of a tail which put him to utter shame wherever he went; for it was soon rumored why he had submitted it to be cut off. The plain females would have nothing to do with him, and though he had lost his tail he had preserved his impudence and tried to intrude himself into respectable rat society as of old.

He met rebuffs everywhere. At last he was forced to the solitary lot of an outcast where he had time to meditate upon the

MORAL :

It is better to be a long-tailed rat among rats than a cotton-tailed rat among rabbits.

THE LUXURIOUS CATS.

A pair of cats, male and female, were introduced into a stylish house on the Avenue, the master saying his premises, especially the barn and carriage house, had been infested with rats.

When this was reported to the rats there was general consternation among them, until one rat who had been a commercial traveler, spoke up and said:

"Be not troubled, my friends, I knew these cats before they came to this house. They will be too well-fed and they are too proud and lazy to catch rats."

"But there is a pair of these cats, male and female," said an old rat, "and I've often noticed that where two cats are living together and are friendly, a litter of kittens soon appear. Alas, I fear we are undone."

"Be not troubled, my friends," said the commercial-traveler rat; "I know this she-cat: she is not the kind of a cat that has kittens."

MORAL :

Luxurious women who refuse to bear children, leave the pestuous part of society to multiply.

THE PULLET AND THE CHICKS.

A pullet, who peculiarly enough, determined she would neither lay eggs nor hatch them out, sought to gather unto herself a brood of young chicks from the eggs and hatchings of other hens.

She declared that neither the hen that layed the egg nor the one that hatched it out was the true mother of the chick.

She claimed that the hen that hovered the chicks and cared for them and fed them and taught them to behave becomingly, was the true mother of the chicks.

So after a deal of persuasion she induced several motherly old hens to let her have several of their chicks to prove her theories. But when she began to go away with them and to hunt and scratch for them, she found the chicks soon ran back to their respective mothers.

With disappointment and humiliation she went to a proud old cock who had often tried to persuade her to become his wife, and asked him why the chicks abandoned her.

He stepped about and crowed lustily two or three times before answering her, and then said:

"You cannot be a mother and remain a pullet. You did not cluck right."

MORAL:

Kindergartners and schoolmams cannot be mothers by proxy.

THE GENIE AND THE VALLEY.

There was once a beautiful valley. There was waving grain in the fields, and in the meadows were happy harvesters, and in the pastures were herds of kine grazing. And there were hedges where wild roses grew, and old fences and gates by the woodlands; and there were farm houses and barns and villages. And in every house in all that valley a pair of sweethearts lived. And there were children going to school swinging their baskets. And there were lovers walking near the shaded nooks and by the still waters.

Travelers came from all the world to

look upon this beautiful valley, for they said: "Here man seems to be a part of nature."

In the mountains which surrounded this beautiful valley, lived a Genie. And it was his habit to come and sit upon a cliff in the evening and look upon that valley.

One evening as he sate˙ there was a frown upon his brow, and there was a fierce look in his eyes and a curl about his nostrils. And after a while, the frown and the curl about his nostrils changed to a smile—but his eyes were yet searching and lit by a strange, hard light.

Then he said unto himself: "I will build me a temple in this valley. I will mix my mortar with blood, and sweat, and tears. The solid parts shall be mixed of human flesh and bones, and the draperies shall be woven of human hair, some of youth, some of woman, some of manhood, and some of the silvered time of age.

The sounds of the trowel and of the hammer, and the music and echo of its domes shall be of sighs and groans, and the weepings of partings; and the silence of its arches shall be the silences of resignation and of despair."

So the Genie came down into the valley and took the disguise of a great merchant, and that same glint was in his eyes.

And he caused the farmer to bring his products unto him, and the housewife to bring hers; and the mechanic to bring his; and the shepherd to bring his; and the weavers who wrought at the looms, to bring theirs; and the miner to bring his;

and the hunter to bring his; and he sent men in distant ships to bring the fruits and products of every clime unto him; he sent men down to sea, and down under the sea to bring up trophies. And every hand of skill and every brain of cunning in all that valley he turned to his service.

And it happened that the farmer did not whistle across his fields as of old; and the housewife did not hum and sing about her work; the mechanic did not meet his wife with a smile nor toss his children; the shepherd ceased his piping; the weavers bent lower and their thinner fingers flew faster; the miner dug deeper and some never came out of the mines; and the hunter went hungry and .cold; and those who went in ships wept at parting but never came back; and some that went under the sea never came up; the angel of death often stayed the hand of the artist; and the brains of cunning grew weary and went wild with raving.

And some had their fingers cut off; and of some he took a hand and of others both arms; and some gave a leg and some both legs; and some gave their teeth; and some gave one eye and some both eyes; and some gave their hearing; and others had their bodies crushed; some died of hunger and some of disease; and some did crimes, and some did thefts to bring goods unto the Genie. And of some he took their honor; and some gave up love; and some could not marry the ones they loved; and babes perished because their mothers forgot them. And many gave their hair; and women gave their beauty; some gave their youth; and some tore the jewels from their ears and from their breasts and the rings from their fingers and gave him.

And some wept, and some cursed, and some prayed when they had nothing left. And some who had lovers and were more beautiful than all the rest, gave up their bodies to him; and of these he made the caryatids which supported the arches of his temple; and of all the rest of the things that were brought him he builded his temple; and when it was finished he laughed, and he said:

"Behold, I shall have renown."

And the people looked and wondered, and they said: "How great and good is he who builded the temple;" and they went in and admired the arches and domes and halls and colonnades, but they could not see what the mortar and the solid walls and the draperies were made of.

THE WAITING BUZZARDS.

A group of buzzards were seated upon the branches of a dead tree near a field, watching the progress of a combat between a bull and a horse.

"Why are you gathered together so quietly," said a passing eagle to the buzzards.

"We expect from appearances," said the buzzards, "to soon have the pleasure of devouring one or two carcasses."

MORALS:

1. The wise benefit by the conflict of fools.

2. The infidels watching the conflict betweeen Roman Catholics and Protestants.

THE DEVIL, THE GOD AND THE MAN.

A devil once pursued a man around the margin of a small lake. The devil was afraid of water and could not cross the lake, so that the man easily avoided him by keeping on the opposite side.

The man was becoming very tired of being chased, when to his joy he saw a god approach the devil. "Now," said the man, "being enemies, they will surely engage each other while I can make my escape."

But to his surprise he heard them agree between themselves to one go one way and the other the other way around the lake, and first catch the man, after which they could as well fight out their ancient quarrel.

MORAL:

The Romanists and Protestants uniting to pursue the liberty of conscience to its destruction.

THE DOGS AND THE PEASANT.

An honest peasant carrying a basket of meat and vegetables, was going home across a field when two packs of hungry dogs, one from either side of the field, set after him with great fierceness.

The man in his fright wisely took timely refuge upon a haystack in the middle of the field. The dogs surrounded the stack, and so certain were they of getting the man that the two packs began to fight each other, each pack claiming him as its rightful prey.

Seeing this the man hissed them on,- and to such good effect, that the two packs had soon worried each other so they could hardly move; and the man came down and went safely home about his business.

MORAL:

The modern infidels pursued by the Romanists and the Protestants.

THE CUNNING THIEF.

A group of men once set a pack of dogs to pursue a thief who took to his heels through a forest.

When the dogs came up to the thief he cunningly hissed them on in the direction they were going; they mistaking him for one of their masters. When their masters came up and the dogs returned from their fruitless pursuit it was found the thief had swiftly effected his escape in another direction.

MORAL:

The cunning of the wicked often defeats the good intent of the means of justice.

EXPERIENCE AGAINST TEARS.

A man who had remained a bachelor until forty, finally married; and one day in an altercation his wife sought to gain her point by resorting to tears. At this he took his hat and cane and walked out of the house, saying:

"My dear, when a bachelor I learned to beware of a woman with a tear in her eye."

The Sheep and the Shepherd.

An old ram who was always marauding through distant fields and woods, complained to the shepherd of the thorns plucking and robbing him of his wool.

"If you stay at home in the open pasture," said the shepherd, "you will have no cause to complain. The thorns pluck the wool from the roaming sheep."

The next day the shepherd in passing through the wood saw the birds gathering the wool from the thorns to build their nests.

"Ah," said he, "the roaming sheep hath his uses; for nature compensates the loss of one by the gain of another."

EVERY TREE LEANS.

A woodman and his son went into the forest to fell trees. Having decided to cut down a certain tree, the son asked his father on which sides he should cut the notches.

"It will fall easiest," said the man, "in the direction toward which it leans. Every tree leans a little; every tree has its way to fall."

MORAL:
Every character has its weaker side.

THE POISONED RATS.

A man whose house had become infested with rats, having tried in vain to trap or bane them, hit upon the happy expedient of pretending to eat from a bowl of porridge himself, while at the same time he mixed a goodly portion of poison in it. He then left it on the table accessible to the rats.

As the drove came out into the kitchen to forage at night, one wise old rat warned the rest to beware of the bowl of porridge which he averred was left too easy of access to be above suspicion; but when one of the younger rats declared he had seen no less a person than the master of the house himself eating from that very porridge just where it sat, they all pitched in and ate of it greedily.

When the pains began to strike them, they all cried in dismay: "Alas, we are undone. He has tricked us at last."

As they were burning with thirst, some proposed rushing out and plunging into the brook.

"Stay, my friends," cried the old rat. "We must all die anyhow, so let us make him pay as dearly as possible for our lives; we will remain and die in the house; every rat to his hole."

MORAL:

A very human trait of character. The woman who brings a scandalous breach of promise suit.

THE CONCEITED DONKEY.

A donkey once imagined himself to be one of great wisdom; and with all sincerity deported himself with such a countenance and manner that many of the other animals of the fields and forests were undecided among themselves as to the justice of his claims of wisdom.

When he found that he had excited this interest among them, he one day sat himself up in judgment and bade the other animals come about him to be instructed.

At this many of the other animals gathered around him; some in mirth, some in ridicule, some out of curiosity, and some suspecting he might be truly wise.

He claimed that none of them knew their own calling. "For examples," he said: "the squirrel does not know how to run up a tree; the bull does not know how to twist a bush; the duck does not know how to swim."

In attempting to instruct the squirrel he tried to run up a tree, but skinned his nose against the trunk and fell back on the ground and broke his tail, so that it stuck up and out to one side; in showing the bull how to twist a bush, he set his long ears for horns and attacking a thorn-bush, soon made them bleed and scratched out one of his eyes; in showing the duck how to swim, he jumped from a high bank into a deep pond and was soon drowned.

"The world is well rid of the conceited ass," said the animals.

MORAL:

Do not try to teach other people their own business.

THE BREACHY COW.

A farmer bought an old cow which a neighbor was willing to sell for what seemed a cheap price.

Having turned her into the pasture with his other cattle, he found to his surprise the next morning that she had pushed down the fence and let the entire herd into his cornfield, where they had wrought great damage.

Seeing this he removed the cow from among the herd and confined her in a high enclosure whence it was impossible for her to escape : but, to his dismay, the next morning, the entire herd was again in the cornfield.

"Alas," said the farmer; "the old cow was dear at any price, for she has taught my entire herd to be breachy."

MORAL:

Keep evil persons from among the innocent and good.

For example: If you have a sweet, virtuous, innocent wife, do not let her come in contact with the experienced, secret-telling, "breachy" woman. Those who fall are generally first vitiated in their minds and imaginations by persons of their own sex.

The woman who says: "Oh, I know all about men, and I have no confidence in any of them," is the "breachy cow."

THE COWS AND THE BULLS.

The cows once sent a committee of their number to the farmer to petition him to adopt the same rules for the bulls as for themselves; saying that the one huge bull the farmer had provided to associate with them, was entirely too lordly and too privileged a character to suit their ideas of equality and propriety.

The farmer being a man of kind heart but weak judgment, consented to carry out any arrangement they might suggest.

Pleased at their success, they suggested that the male calves be treated so they would grow exactly like the females in size and qualities; and that the door of the barn should be made only large enough to pass the larger sized cows, which would of course be large enough for the " equal-rights " bulls.

(NOTE. It is a fact in nature that bulls grow to be twice as large as cows.)

When the fourth spring-time came and the door was opened, and the cattle all permitted to go out to pasture for the season, it was found the bulls had grown so large, that it was impossible for them to pass the door.

The cows went on to the range without them, but in a few days they again sent their committee to the farmer, saying:

"Nature is not to be thwarted. We pray you to enlarge the door of the barn. We prefer to sacrifice our philosophy rather than forego the society of the bulls."

A few of the cows soon smarted under this defeat, saying:

"If we can't cause the bulls to be like cows, we can at least imitate the bulls, and claim for ourselves as many privileges as they."

So at evening when the herd came home, these cows went bellowing and fighting and pawing the dust, and twisting bushes that stood in their way. They disowned their calves, refused to be milked, and in many ways deported themselves in such manner that the milk-maids fled in terror, declaring to the farmer that those cows had gone stark mad.

"How ridiculous they have made themselves," said the farmer, "by their foolish notions in regard to the equality of the sexes. We will drive them to-morrow to the butcher."

The other cows and the bulls felt alike ashamed of and sorry for them, as they were driven away.

MORAL:

Women who clamor for equal privileges for the sexes.

FATE'S TRUE LOVE.

A TRUE ROMANCE.

I was walking along a country road in romantic Switzerland meditatively humming:

"Oh, love is a flower,
 Blooming now for me;"

When suddenly a white dove fluttered down upon my shoulder. Recovering from my surprise I found a small white envelope on the ground at my feet. Following the dove with my eye I noticed it swiftly wing to the welcoming hand of a little girl, perhaps fourteen years of age, who sat upon a hill beyond the hedge a quarter of a mile away.

I lifted my hat and bowed, and she

tossed her white kerchief once and then resumed caressing the dove.

On opening the envelope I found a delicate Swiss flower resembling our arbutus, and read in very good French, this legend:

"I know thee not,
But yet I love thee."

I was four thousand miles from home and younger then by many a year. Only those who have felt the callousing prints of time can realize how tender and romantic the heart is at twenty. Time but makes early impressions deeper. Time treads lightly upon the hardened sand.

At the station whither I was going, I received important mail and dispatches, which notified me of the necessity of my immediate return to America, and to my home in Cincinnati. But, before leaving, I inquired of the Village Master the name of the little girl who inhabited the pretty hillside cottage I had passed. He told me she was the daughter of a French officer, banished during the troublous reign of the last Napoleon.

He stated she had trained a dove to deliver a message, when liberated, to the nearest human being in sight. Then I knew I was by fate or accident, if not by the girl's intention, the rightful recipient of the message.

Her name was Elza De Vere; address, Vevay, Environne.

I believe in love and I believe in fate, and so do you, fair reader.

* * * * * *

Five years had passed. I had entered business in Cincinnati. Among my employes was a young girl who, every morning, brought with her to my factory a white dove, which she kept imprisoned until noon, at which time she liberated it to carry a message to her mother. It was a beautiful and tender thing for this humble girl to do. This was realizing the old legend of doves carrying love messages. All the poets from Anacreon to Moore had sung of it. The prisoner in his cell both in real life and upon the mimic stage had used the messenger dove to communicate with friends or lover.

With a sigh on my lips and a sob in my heart, I thought of the little Swiss girl; for I was still sentimental at twenty-five. The very landscape, the fresh June meadows, the hillside, the pretty cottage; all came vividly before me. I remembered she must be nearly twenty now, and I imagined her still as innocent and pure as the flower she sent me by her white dove. Curiosity and something in my heart, I did not then understand, made me wish and ponder and wonder. I was of that age when we feel sure that somewhere in the world our ideal lover or sweetheart lives and waits for our coming.

Sometimes we catch a glimpse of a noble or pretty face walking from us and wonder, fear it is our ideal love walking away from us. We are almost tempted to disregard formality and speak without an introduction. We all believe in eyes which look love to eyes which speak again.

Opening my desk, I took from its place my long-neglected commonplace book of European notes. And when I found there the little girl's address and the very envelope and the faded flower the dove had thrown at my feet; and when I read

"I know thee not,
But yet I love thee."

I believed, feared, hoped that my ideal

love, intended for me by fate and awaiting my coming, was Elza De Vere, Vevay, Environne, Switzerland.

* * * * * *

I seized my pen and wrote to her a short impassioned letter; I say impassioned, but passion burned between the lines more than in the words. It was worded diplomatically so that a Platonic construction could have been put upon it if it had proved Elza had forgotten me.

Reason sometimes whispered to me that it was improbable she should have remembered a stranger, and the, to her, perhaps trivial incident.

But a spell was over me and it grew upon me. I could not sleep except at irregular intervals. I took long drives or rambles at night in parks or on drear and lonely highways. Often the morning moon glistened on my oar upon the silent rippling river before the steam whistles had awaked, and while the ghosts of greed and traffic still hovered over the sullen docks. Something whispered to me; something haunted my heart; and I was sure it was the waiting, suffering love of Elza De Vere.

I counted the days and estimated the very hour she would receive my letter. How I wished she would cable me a message. I believed she would; I could feel with an intensity amounting almost to a sensation that she would cable me. I left orders at my hotel that I should be immediately notified if a message came, day or night. Something seemed impending; something somewhere seemed to fill me with a mysterious dread: I met a priest upon the street and involuntarily shrank from him. I did not then know why.

A messenger boy came. I was dressed

and waiting. I signed his book with a trembling hand. It was a cable message, and read as follows :

> My father dead, leaving great wealth. Jesuits will conceal me in a cloister to secure it. I have waited so long for you. I love you. Will try to escape to-night and sail for America. On earth and in heaven I am yours.
> ELZA DE VERE.

* * * * * * *

In this cablegram my intuitive hopes and fears were strangely realized. All the slow years of my blindness and neglect rushed upon me in a few moments and o'erwhelmed me.

The clock upon a neighboring church tower struck seven, and I shuddered. I calculated the difference of longitude and the difference of time and knew that the clock of the accursed tower in Switzerland was at that moment striking midnight. Would my love, could she, escape? I knew at that moment she was either a writhing, innocent prisoner, or a fleeing fugitive hastening, like her own white dove, to the home and protection of her lover.

Did I dare to cable a message? It could not reach there till morning, and would it not fall into the hands of her villainous captors and hasten the consummation of their plot? I studied the words of her message and the varied possibilities they suggested. I decided to cable the Burgomaster of Vevay as follows:

Help Elza De Vere. Notify her I am coming.

I could not get a train to New York until morning. I did not sleep that night. As midnight struck, I knew the unsympathizing morning sun was tipping with light the hills of Switzerland. Would the twelve hours of my waiting never wear away.

I sat down and, quietly closing my eyes,

tried to put my thoughts in communication with Elza De Vere by that method of mysterious mind-telegraph the psychologists have written about. Her soul seemed to answer to mine that she was in durance and in despair, yet hoping for my coming. It was maddening.

I arose and swept it away as a disorder of my own imagination. In tranquil reason and in action by such slow means as the world afforded was my only hope.

Ten days at least, without accident, would be required for me to reach the little Swiss village. How I hated the breadth of the Atlantic; how I wished for wings. I almost wished my soul were free from its clay, that it might speed like a thought to the rescue of my love. I would have fought, but I could only have beaten the air. I would have prayed, but I am an infidel to the god of the priests. Hope kept me from despair, and when the slow morning came, I was first at the station.

* * * * * * *

Before setting sail from New York, I made arrangements for the reception and comfort of Elza De Vere should she be so fortunate as to escape and arrive in America before my return. Once on the deep I had time for reflection. How tardily the slow monarch seemed to paw its way among the waves. I importuned the captain to assure me of the earliest probable hour of our arrival at Liverpool. How eagerly I watched every west-bound sail, hoping my love might be safely on board. I had left orders in New York to cable me the moment she arrived, in which event I would return immediately.

From Liverpool I sped to the continent, thence to Switzerland. I sought the Burgomaster, who handed me my own cable message to him. It had arrived the morning after I sent it. He stated he had sought the cottage of Elza De Vere, but found it locked and abandoned. The furniture remained the same as if the occupants had only gone away on a temporary absence. The next evening it was burned to the ground, with all the contents.

I hastened to the spot and found nothing but cold, damp ashes. I searched for the slightest clew, but in vain. I found an unlettered peasant who remembered that after her father's death Elza had been taken away at night by some strange doctors, to restore her health, which, they stated, had been greatly affected by her grief. I offered a reward amounting to all my fortune, and spent a year in Europe searching for a possible clew to her whereabouts. She never arrived in America.

I returned to Cincinnati and quietly resumed my business. For several years I harbored a steadily fading hope that in some way my love would sometime be able to make herself known to me.

Fifteen years have passed. I am forty and still a bachelor. Many of my readers may have often seen me upon the streets, sometimes in public places, rarely in ladies' society; a quiet business man, aging rapidly, living sometimes at one hotel and then at another. I have often been rallied for remaining a bachelor, to which I generally make a reply of some pleasantry. But I have never before related this—a true story of an incident in my life.

The reader can answer my life's problem as well as I. Was I or was I not robbed of Fate's true love by the duplicity of avaricious priests?

SUPPLEMENTARY PREFACE.

As the printing of this book proceeds, I find that (having several other books in manuscript) I've got the wrong preface to the wrong book, and take occasion here to set myself right.

Nearly every thing in this book (including the preface) was written within the last four months, prior to its publication; indeed the printer has taken much of it wet, (yes, that's a good expression) wet from my pen.

And while I'm unexpectedly out again before the curtain to make additional prefatory bows, I want to beg the reader to not judge my book by any single part of it; be easy on me in certain spots. Perhaps I, myself, am as good an illustration of some of the fables and other points as the reader is.

There is one thing that gives me a few twinges of conscience; and that is, my book will hurt the feelings of some well-intending readers; but I couldn't *hold the book in* any longer, as I explained on pages three and four; and that is the very reason I'm bowing and bobbing around so much in this preface. The more I think on it, the more my conscience twinges like a fiddle string; and worse and worse, the book is likely to live—yes, actually live—and be read after I'm dead and gone—and generations yet unborn may have their feelings hurt. What right have I to so afflict them? Alas! I have but one excuse: I couldn't help it; they will simply be unfortunate in not having lived and died before I did.

I wish I knew at this writing whether there are any more fables and such things in me or not; for I expect this is the last chance I'll have to apologize; and if I only knew, I could decide how to act. But I begin to suspect I have, unlike other authors, made the mistake of writing my preface before instead of after writing my book. This circumstance proves my innocence, and shows their books to be little short of premeditated villainy.

Have you noticed how seriously most authors take themselves and their books? They accuse the public of being afflicted with a long-felt want which their books are intended to fill; but in nearly all cases the long-felt want is painfully close to the anatomy of the author himself.

Another peculiarity, common to authors, preachers and legislators, is their claim that they believe they are trying to do good to the public; whereas everybody else knows that if these same self-constituted good-doers would shut up shop for at least twenty years, and give the real newspapers, the theaters and the Fine Arts a chance, it would be the greatest public blessing since the discovery of America. What loads of expense it would lift from the people—especially from the poor, upon whom such burdens eventually fall.

But do not imagine I'm not taking my own book seriously; for if I do not, who will?

THE AUTHOR.

(See " The Author and the Reader," page 221.)

BOY TALK.

ADDRESS TO THE BOYS OF THE WAIF'S MISSION, CHICAGO.

I want to talk to the hearty, rough-and-tumble boys, who don't wear knee breeches nor Little Lord Fauntleroy collars and cuffs. The shorter the boy's hair is the better I like the boy too.

Every boy has had a mother, and nearly every boy has had a father, some time in his life; and don't you forget it. Every Mission boy had a mother; and don't you forget her, boys. You may not have known her; but somebody knew her. She may have been a young and beautiful girl.

She was pure and innocent too; as pure as the roses you sometimes see growing in the gardens of the rich. Nearly every boy's mother loved him when he was a helpless, dimpled babe. Every baby is beautiful and sweet in the eyes of its own mother. I don't care how rough and tough some of you boys are now; you were once a little dimpled baby, in a loving mother's arms. She loved you too; and don't you forget it. Once I saw a waif standing observing a beautiful young woman as she passed. As he turned away he murmured to himself, "I wonder if my mother was like her."

The life of every one of you is connected with a romance; and could it be told, would be a more thrilling novel than the story-tellers tell. Connected with you boys are tales of love, of hope, of struggle, of wrong, of suffering, of shame, of heartbreak and despair. There are stories of trust, of oppression, of starvation and temptation beyond endurance. There are paths touched by your young lives where pride and shame, comedy and tragedy, life and death, walk hand in hand.

A few days ago, in that bad city by the sea, a young mother carried a beautiful boy baby in her arms on the street. She was almost starved, and daily being dragged into shame. Her babe kept her from securing honorable employment; and rather than see it and herself perish of want, she thought to abandon it in a hallway, to be found by some more fortunate person. She put her boy down upon the floor; and as she went out she turned to take a last look, and saw him primp his pretty lips and cry. Haunted by that look and cry she could not go two rods upon the street, but hastened back to pacify him by kisses and caresses, amid her own tears. Again she left him; when she looked back he smiled. She could not go; and again rushed to clasp him in her arms. Now she opened her breast and nursed him to sleep. Carefully she laid him on the floor, and went on tip-toe out into the street. But she remembered the sweet, placid face of her sleeping babe, and her breasts were still moist from his lips. Again she rushed back, fearing some one had found him; and clasping him in her arms, exclaimed, " I cannot; I cannot; now I will never leave him!"

With her babe in her arms she was returning to the street to resume fighting a harder battle than ever a soldier faced.

But another woman happened to come down the stairs and witness this last act of the tragedy. She called a policeman, and had the mother arrested for attempting to abandon her babe. The mother and babe were imprisoned for the crime.

No, boys; she was imprisoned for winning a victory in the hardest battle in which the human heart was ever engaged.

Now, boys, I want to tell you a fable of

THE YOUNG ROBINS.

The Father-robin had been shot by the sportsman; so the Mother-robin had to leave the nest with five helpless young ones in it, and go abroad among the fields and furrows to hunt food for them.

At last, after a long search of turning over chips and stones, and looking under clods, here, there, and everywhere, she was compelled to return, almost famishing herself, with but a single morsel of food for her young.

As her light wing and foot were felt upon the rim of the nest, five slender necks, with open mouths, were eagerly stretched up to receive the expected nourishment.

"Alas, my darlings!" said she; "in the fields and furrows of the farmer no worms or grains are to be found. I am almost starving myself. My wings are so weak they can hardly carry me. I have secured for you only a single morsel of food. If I give it to one of you, I fear the others will perish before I can find more."

Higher than ever and more eagerly the five helpless necks and mouths were stretched, and each one cried:

"O mother, give it to me."

"My darlings," she said, "I cannot choose among you. I am glad your eyes are not yet open. You cannot see my wretchedness. As your eyes are blind, so shall mine be."

So saying, she closed her eyes, and fed some one of the open mouths, and flew away. When she returned only one open mouth was held up to her. And then she knew which one she had fed!

Boys, each of you may have been the young robin that got your mother's last morsel of food.

There are only a few things in this world worth much.

The greatest of all these is to have a mother. Don't forget yours, boys; and remember she was a far better woman than the men or women who robbed her.

The next best thing is to love and be loved by a woman. With this, a home is possible; without it, a home is not possible. Some people imagine a house with persons living in it is a home. In every true home a pair of sweethearts live.

I know an old bachelor who has an income of fifteen thousand dollars a year without much labor; but he has no home. He is more homeless than you Mission boys are. He owns houses, and can travel anywhere in the world he wishes; but the more he goes, the more homeless he is. Money can't make a home.

I know an old Chinaman who has a nice Chinese wife and six babies. She does the washing, and he does the ironing, for their small laundry. But they are happy; and you ought to see how bright the black eyes of those six children are! They have a home. They live in Washington; and, when I saw them, I said: "They are happier than the president."

Many persons who live in fine houses on the avenues have no homes; they are only boarding with their servants.

Now, boys, I don't want you to make

any promises to me or to anybody else; but I wish each one of you would form a resolution in your own mind to have a home of your own just as soon as possible. You can have a home soon too; all your very own. Don't try to be governor or president. They often have the gout or dyspepsia; their heads don't lie easy on their pillow at night, either. Don't say much about it; but you just resolve in your own mind to be an honest, gentle, home-making man. That's the best and greatest thing to be.

I know a very wealthy woman in Chicago who gives many grand "receptions;" she is getting old now, and I have found out that in her heart she would give all her diamonds and silks and wealth for one gentle word from her husband, or for one cooing smile of a baby of her own.

I take it that each boy who reads this has already resolved to not always be a waif, but to have a home of his own; and I want to tell you a couple of things about how to have this home. You must always say "our" in speaking about your home, with one exception. You can say "my wife;" but about everything else you must say *our*. Say, *our* house, *our* home, *our* children, *our* money, *our* horses. I never saw a happy home where the man kept saying "my" about everything.

I also take it that every boy who has resolved to have a home of his own knows he will have a wife; and before I stop talking, I want to tell you one or two things about how to treat a wife; and remember, no woman is any good to you except she is your wife.

Have you ever noticed a woman's

hands and eyes, and her hair and skin; how delicate and tender they are? She is of finer mould and texture than you or men are; and just so she is more gentle, delicate, and tender in her heart and feelings than you are. Boys, I charge you to be gentle with your wife. You may have it rough-and-tumble out in the world, but when you go into your home, be gentle; otherwise you will drive love out, and then your happy home will be broken.

Now, I wonder if anybody has before talked to you about the same things I have. It seems to me the greatest defect of present-day education that boys and girls are not taught how to be husbands and wives, fathers and mothers, and makers of true, happy homes.

The Puppy and Experience.

———o———

A half-grown puppy went into the fields and woodlands to walk alone for the first time. As he passed along the edge of a cliff, the sun being low, his body, legs, and tail cast a very large shadow upon the valley.

"Heigh-ho!" he exclaimed, observing his shadow; "how I have grown! I am larger than the largest elephant I ever heard of. But it is undignified for me to be trotting and bobbing along like this. Large bodies move slowly."

With this, he began to step high and slowly, at the same time watching the dignified movements of his shadow.

Presently he noticed a bull grazing in the meadow below; and he said to himself:

"I'll just go down and astonish that bull by stepping upon him, and crushing him to the ground."

So, after a parting, admiring glance at his shadow, he fixed his eyes steadily upon the bull, and with profound dignity of step and manner, as he supposed, descended to the valley, and approached the bull.

The bull did not notice the approach of the puppy until it was quite near, when he suddenly turned and tossed it high in the air over his back.

The puppy fell near a brook, wherein he saw his image at its true size. After he found out where he was, and recalled the direction home, he limped away, saying:

"It is in the mirror of experience, after all, that we can justly estimate ourselves."

A Man and His Trowsers.

A poor man once had two pairs of trowsers; but each pair was full of holes. Happily, it happened that the holes in one pair were not in the same places the holes in the other pair were; so that by wearing both pairs at once, he declared himself as well protected from the cold as anybody.

Morals:

1. The makeshifts of the poor often counterbalance the providence of the rich.

2. Two hurts in one place wound us deeply indeed.

THE WOMEN WHO SAW A GOD.

---o---

Not often in modern times have the supernatural beings of the universe interposed in behalf of humans; but there is one well-authenticated instance which, owing to the humor of the persons concerned, has never been mentioned. It was during the twenty-third Administration of the Republic. It was at the Capital, in the parlors of the principal hotel.

The wives of senators had gathered there in order to "receive," as it was called in those days. A god was present in the form of a magnificent painting which hung upon the wall. Many admired the painting, but no one knew it was a god.

The miracle occurred when there were none present except the senators' wives and one other. All were arrayed in their costliest raiment, and they were chatting, and assuming the superiority they felt fate had conferred upon them. Presently, some seemed to hear distant, delicious music; but at first some could not hear it. And those who heard looked one toward another, and in different directions, and at the ceiling, and listened; and as the music grew louder, all began to hear it. And some declared in awed whispers that they saw the picture raise its eyes and look on them, and that there was a circle of light about its head. And even yet none knew it was a god; but all thought it some peculiar favor of art, due to their own high station.

At this moment the door opened, and

the colored wife of a colored senator and her sister entered, to pay their respects to the assembled women; but the women stood astonished, and with disdain, that one of another race, though of equal rank, should essay to approach their presence. All stood in haughty reserve; and the colored women waited embarrassed near the door. Some of the women turned their backs, and some sent scornful glances toward the embarrassed colored women who stood waiting for recognition near the door.

Then all heard the music again, and saw the halo about the head of the picture. And when the women looked one toward the other, they saw that the face and neck and arms and hands of each were turning black; and each one looked at her own hands and arms, and at her image in the large mirrors, and saw that she was black. And they all turned and looked toward the waiting women near the door, and saw that they were white. And the waiting women looked in astonishment, and saw that the assembled senators' wives were black; and the two waiting women looked at each other, and each saw that the other was white. And they blushed, and were still more embarrassed. And then they heard the music too, and saw the halo about the head of the picture; and they were so embarrassed that they withdrew out through the door whence they had come.

And the senators' wives looked at each other, and saw themselves turning white again. And when they listened for the music again, they heard it not; and when they looked for the picture, it had vanished from the wall.

And as they went home, each one

heard something whispering in her ears which no one else could hear, and which she vainly tried to silence by putting her fingers in her ears, and by talking very loud to her companions.

And no one has spoken of this miracle unto this day.

The Fox and the Wood-Duck.

A sly old fox was one day taking a walk when he espied a wood-duck building her nest upon the ground amid some brambles.

"Heigh-ho!" said he to himself; "if I am wise I'll wait until there are young ones in that nest, and then I'll make a meal of both the mother and her brood."

He peered through the brambles very stealthily, lest he should alarm the wood-duck, and set her to flight, well knowing that after she had finished her nest she would not be so easy to leave it.

He was just sneaking away without even shaking a twig, when he noticed a bright-hued, quick-witted pheasant approach and accost the wood-duck.

The fox crouched flat, and listened with all his ears; for he knew that pheasants are as wise and witty as they are beautiful.

He overheard the pheasant advise the wood-duck that it was dangerous to build her nest upon the ground for fear of becoming the prey of foxes and other varmints that are always prowling around. " Besides," continued the pheasant, " all the wood-ducks of my acquaintance are building their nests high up in the trees this season ; it is the new fashion of the best grade of duck society."

The pheasant flew away, leaving the wood-duck about decided to abandon the ground and build her nest in the trees.

"The jig is up with my scheme," said the fox to himself, as he crept away unseen and unheard; " the jig is up, unless I can persuade her to remain upon the ground. Now for a test of my cunning."

He now made his way far around, to approach the duck from another direction; and in order to not alarm her, he resolved to pretend to be sorely wounded. He put a bandage over one eye, and tied one foot up, so as to limp along on three legs.

"Good-day, Mrs. Wood-Duck," said he, with a half-smile at her, and a half-grimace of pain at his own condition.

"Good-day, sir," said the wood-duck, but slightly alarmed.

"I see you are building a very nice nest there in that delightful place," said he.

"This is my first season, and I'm not much used to building nests, sir," said she, pleased at his remark.

"Your first season, indeed? You build it just as your good old mother did hers. I knew her very well, good madam," said he.

"I do the best I can, sir," said she; "and I was quite satisfied with it until Miss Pheasant, who flew away a few minutes ago, advised me that it is the latest fashion to build nests in trees; besides, she thought a nest on the ground was in danger from marauding enemies at night. It must be very dark here on the ground at night, sir."

"Pooh! the vain, silly thing! What does Miss Pheasant know about ducks' nests, anyhow? I think if your good old mother didn't know how to build nests and where to build them, it's not for the like of Miss Pheasant to teach her. Besides, how could your enemies see you or your nest in the darkness of the night? And how would you get your young down to the ground when once they were hatched in the lofty trees? They might fall out and break their precious necks. Poor little dears!" said he with great show of emotion.

"I'm sure I don't know what is best," said she.

"I am astonished, Mrs. Wood-Duck," said he, "that you should depart from the ways of your dear old mother. Alas! the ingratitude of the rising generation! You wouldn't do such a thing, would you, now? Your poor old mother would turn over in her grave if she knew you did such a thing."

He could plainly see that Mrs. Wood-Duck was greatly affected; and as he limped away he gleefully and rightly decided she would finish building her nest right where she had begun it. In due season he enjoyed the feast he originally planned.

MORAL:

The Roman Catholics persuading young persons to remain in the Church because their mothers were Roman Catholics.

Do They Remember?

———o———

The flowers she wore on her breast that
    day;
    Do they remember?
Will they bloom for me in the heart of
    May?
    Or in December?
Did they hear and know, and what would
    they say?
She wore them for me on her breast that
    day;
    Do they remember?
With their lips of pink, and their eyes of
    blue,
    Do they remember?
What do they know? could they tell it to
    you?

Do they remember?
Would they dare to tell what they saw and heard?
Could they tell of her blushes and one sweet word?
Do they remember?

NEVER A DREAM.

Never a dream of the heart or the brain,
That once thrilled the pulse, but will thrill it again;
Never a love of the pure and the true,
But will cling to the heart and the memory too.

My Harp and I.

———o———

I sang to my Harp one morning in June,
   And listened to hear its reply;
For each word of my song came a note of
      my tune,
   As I listened to hear its reply.
      But its strings are now broken,
      And I know by this token,
" Farewell " was the word of its sigh.
      And I know by this token,
      As if by words spoken,
" Farewell " was the word of its sigh.

I sang to the orchard, to the blossoming
      trees,
   And listened to hear their reply ;
I heard my song echoed in the hum of the
      bees,

As I listened to hear their reply.
But December is coming,
And I knew by their humming,
" Farewell" was their word of reply.
And I knew by this token,
As if by words spoken,
" Farewell" was their word of reply.

I sang to a robin, just building her nest,
And listened to hear her reply.
She sang my sweet song from the red on
her breast,
As I listened to hear her reply.
But I knew by her singing
She soon would be winging
Her flight to a far-away clime.
And I knew by this token,
As if by words spoken,
" Farewell" was her word of reply.

I sang to my Love, that morning in June,
And listened to hear her reply.
With a smile and a tear she answered my
tune,

As I listened to hear her reply.
But our love is now broken,
And I know by this token,
" Farewell" was the word of her sigh.
And I know by this token,
As if by words spoken,
" Farewell" was the word of her sigh.

I sang to the wide world, that morning in June,
And listened to hear its reply.
The earth and the sky all answered my tune,
As I listened to hear its reply.
But the days will grow colder,
And my life will grow older;
" Farewell" was the word of my sigh ;
And I know by this token,
As if by words spoken,
" Farewell" was its word of reply.

[Music by the author to the above words will be sent post-paid for ten cents by the publishers.]

There Was Love in Her Eyes.

There was love in her eyes that day,
    Jamie ;
There was love in her eyes that day;
As plain as words could have told it,
    Jamie,
There was love in her heart for me.
But now, alas ! there's never a glance, —
    Never a tell-tale e'e.
Unhappy I as time drags by ;
    There's never a glance for me.

I remember her eyes that day, Jamie ;
    It is all I have left, 'tis true ;
But I'd give this world, and all of it,
    Jamie,
If she'd glance as she used to do.
For now, alas ! there's never a glance, —
    Never a tell-tale e'e.

Unhappy I as time drags by ;
   There's never a glance for me.

I cannot tell why she blames me, Jamie ;
   She was happy, I know, that day ;
She wore my flowers as if proud of them,
     Jamie ;
   But now she has thrown them away.
For now, alas ! there's never a glance, —
   Never a tell-tale e'e.
Unhappy I as time drags by ;
   There's never a glance for me.

Our lives will be drifting apart, Jamie ;
   The world is as wide as that day ;
Will she forget or remember it, Jamie,
   There was love in her eyes for me ?
But now, alas ! there's never a glance, —
   Never a tell-tale e'e.
Unhappy I as time drags by ;
   There's never a glance for me.

[Music by the author to the above words will be sent post-paid by the publishers, for ten cents.]

The Heart of My Sweetheart.

The heart of my sweetheart
  Is a garden with flowers;
  Her love is the roses;
  Her tears are the showers.
  She's pettish, she's bright, —
Like the clouds and the sky;
  She's never quite happy, —
  And neither am I, —
  Unless we are wooing,
  And proposing next June,
  To surely be wedded
When the rose is in bloom.

If she knows her own mind,
  It is more than I know;
  For in winter her garden
  Is covered with snow;

But the sunshine of love
Will melt it like rain,
  And I know that her roses
  Will blossom again;
  For who can tell when
  Her glad springtime shall be
  Or when she will share
Her sweet summer with me?

But the autumn will come,
  When her summer is blown;
  When her love has but ripened,
  And her heart is my own;
  When her fruits are all garnered,—
Her flowers more dear;
  When her love has grown warmer,
  Though the winter is near;
  I'll dream like a traveller
  At rest 'neath her bowers.
  The heart of my sweetheart
Is a garden with flowers.

[Music by the author to the above words will be sent post-paid by the publishers for ten cents.]

The Lover's Lay.

———o———

O Lady fair, my Harp I'll take
   And sing to thee a lover's lay.
My Harp and song I'll ne'er forsake,
   And always sing this lover's lay.

Now, Harp of mine, thy chords awake;
   Thou ne'er hast sighed a sweeter lay.
Come, help me now this song to make;
   Come, help me sing this lover's lay.

O Lady fair, our sweetest song
   My Harp and I to thee will sing.
To thee, the fairest notes belong;
   We'll wake for thee the sweetest string.

Oh, Love is not a transient flower
   That blows and blooms 'neath fairest skies;

'Mid snow and storm, and sun and shower,
   I see it gleam in tranquil eyes.

When fairest eyes and brightest smiles
   Would tempt the heart from thee to rove,
It spurns and scorns such fatal wiles,
   And turns to thee with thoughts of love.

When other joys and friendships woo,
   And round the heart their graces twine,
It sighs alone; it beats for you;
   And whispers: "Thine, Love; only thine."

When sadness rules within the heart,
   And thoughts recall a happier day,
I'll not forget my song and Harp,
   And always sing this lover's lay.

TO . . . .

ON HER FIFTEENTH BIRTHDAY.

Twice seven consenting years had shed
Their grace and gladness o'er thy head.
Sweet childhood's days had scarcely flown;
Sweet childish grace was yet thine own;
When still another summer came,
And left thy heart not quite the same.
Thy cheek more fair, and in thine eyes
The tranquil blue of summer skies;
And something changed thine air and form;
Thy lips more sweet, thy glance more warm.
And if I guess thy riddle well,
Some strange new thought thy heart could tell.
Stay, Cupid, stay thy cruel dart!
Yet spare, oh, spare this maiden heart!

LISTENING LOVE.

———o———

Tell me not in words, sweet Nell,
That your love is mine;
Write it not with golden pen,
Write me not a line;
For well I've known since first we met
That all your love is mine.

I heard it in your voice, sweet Nell,
When once we sang together;
Again as plain as words could tell
When you spoke about the weather;
And well I've known since first we met
That all your love is mine.

You prattled to a babe, sweet Nell,
Upon its mother's knee;

It was the merest nonsense, Nell,
You were telling love to me;
Like music hushed within its shell,
You were telling love to me.

You told it to your bird, sweet Nell,
When I was listening by;
'Twas something in your tones, sweet Nell,
No bird could answer why—
You were telling me your love, sweet Nell,
While I was listening by.

We watched the sunset clouds, sweet Nell,
The moon, the stars, the skies—
You spoke it not aloud, sweet Nell,
I saw it in your eyes;
As plain as words could be, sweet Nell,
I saw it in your eyes.

That night I touched your hand, sweet
    Nell,
'Twas like a fairy's thrill ;
The moon was veiled behind a cloud,
And all the world was still ;
You told me all your love, sweet Nell,
While all the world was still.

To . . . .

———o———

Like a harp that still is sighing
Notes of love and friendship past,
Though the hand that touched it's lying
Far from friends and friendly grasp;

Like a harp that once in gladness
Sang a sweet and joyous strain, —
Joyous then, but now in sadness
Echoes back those notes again;

Like a harp that long hath slumbered,
Waiting for some hand of yore, —
For the hand that once could wake it,
Now, alas! can wake no more:

Thus my heart, from tears and weeping,
Turns again in dreams to thee;
Feigning once again a greeting
Which it knows can never be.

New Year's Greeting.

———o———

You're in my heart to-day, Nell,
And will be all the year;
No word that I could say, Nell,
No thought that is too dear,
That I might not repeat it, Nell,
Through all the glad New Year.

No joy that is too bright, Nell,
No wish that can come true,
No heart that is too light, Nell;
I'd give them all to you.
And if you would but keep it, Nell,
I'd give my Love to you.

MATING-DAY.

———o———

'Tis Mating-Day, sweet Nell, and from the
 skies,
The sunbeams woo the willing earth;
And on the maiden's cheek and in the
 youth's lorn eyes
The love-gleams say: 'Tis Mating-Day.

The soft sea shimmers in a trancing mood;
The buds are bursting to give the blos-
 soms birth;
From every cliff and dale and hill and
 wood
Sings promise of the May: 'Tis Mating-
 Day.

'Tis Mating-Day, sweet Nell, and in thine
 eyes,

And on thy cheek, and on thy lips I see —
Fairer than ev'ry blossom of ev'ry tree,
Sweeter than ev'ry rose of ev'ry clime,
Brighter than ev'ry glow of sunset-time —
The love my soul would live to hear thee
    speak.

To a Young Lady

WHO SENT THE AUTHOR A PIECE OF CAKE MADE BY HER OWN FAIR HANDS.

The cake was so fair, so rich and so rare,
So sweet, so delicious in flavor,
That to judge it aright, in truth, Clara,
    I might
Guess its goodness was caught from its
    maker.

You Touched Me.

———o———

You touched me, Love, and then I knew
That I had lived for none but you;
That all my life, that all my past,
Had trended straight to you at last.

Like fruits that tremble on the bough,
O'er ripe till some sure hand below
Is held to save, then leave the tree,
So from my past I've come to thee.

'Twas like one lost who finds his way;
He cannot doubt, he cannot stay,
But swift on winged feet doth flee;
So swift I came, my Love, to thee.

As sunbeams rest on winter hills,
And melt their snows to summer rills,

That haste away to join the sea,
So melt I, Love, and haste to thee.

Thou art my past, thou art my tree;
I've left them all to cling to thee.
Thy hand hath saved, thy touch set free;
Thou art my sun, thou art my sea.

Thou Art My Sea.

———o———

Thou art my sea, and on thy breast,
I'll trusting sleep and tranquil rest.
When storms shall burst and winds shall
    sweep,
I'll safely hide within thy deep.

When clouds above, like fields of snow,
Shall cast their dark on thee below,
I'll woo the winds to drive away
The shades that dim thy perfect day.

If in thy rage, when tempests roar,
Thou dash me from thee 'gainst the shore,
I'll still consent: "Thou art my sea,"
And, like thy waves, return to thee.

In night's deep dome, — a sea above, —
The starlit sky shall arch our love;
With Love and Faith and Fate in thee
There'll be no death, no other sea.

To a Lady

WHO PRESENTED THE AUTHOR A NECKTIE.

There are silken ties and hempen ties,
And ties of friendship bind us;
But ties that speak through loving eyes —
Bright eyes which still remind us
That angels once to earth were given,
To win our souls from hell to heaven,
And leave all else behind us —
Alas! the ties of loving eyes —
How can they be forgiven?
Without a word, a token,
How can they lift the soul to heaven,
Then leave the heart so broken.

On Seeing a Reptile

FLEE FROM THE PATH OF THE AUTHOR.

Fly not, little reptile! I would not harm thee,
Though dark superstition has made me thy foe.
Let not my presence disturb or alarm thee, —
The rude hand of anger shall deal thee no blow.

Though priests shall deride with fanatical din,
And make thee the emblem of man's basest passion,
Impute to thy wiles the original sin,
In one friendly eye thou shalt meet but compassion.

If a serpent beguiled our first mother, and led her
By the promise of wisdom our woe to begin,
I cannot malign the mild hand that fed her,
Or deny, little reptile, we are brothers in sin.

But aloof let me stand from thy guiltless dominion;
'Tis man's vilest nature has led him awrong : —
Accursed be the fate of fanatic opinion
That has trampled and tortured thy existence so long.

If a few of thy race resent with a sting
The foot that would tread out thy life with its heel,
Thou art not to be loathed as the most wicked thing
Till men are less vile and more tender to feel.

Adieu, little reptile! some hand more unkind
May find thee and slay thee to wreak a revenge
Which the unfeeling hate of an untutored mind
Has heired from a race of degenerate men.

TO A WOMAN

WHO BEGGED THE AUTHOR TO TELL HER OF SOMETHING TO DO.

An artist should not live by, but for, his art. Do not do to live, but live to do. Go out to the world, and the world will come to you; and in just the way and in just the degree you go out to it. Do the first and nearest thing to you, and the next thing, and the next, and the next, will come filing along to be done, just as one person files and pushes after another to shake the hand of a dignitary at a reception.

Pretty soon things to do will come plucking at your elbows; they will catch at you, and cling to your gown as briers do when you pass amid a thicket. Do not fear. If the thorns pluck the wool from the passing sheep, it is for the birds to build their nests; the sheep will never lack for wool.

John Gandy and I.

I wish I could describe what a beautiful opportunity came to me this morning while I was waiting for the train. A bright colored boy approached me, and before I could hardly comprehend it, he had told me in a bashful, innocent way that he was just out of the Cheltenham, Md., Reformatory, where he had spent five years a United States prisoner for stealing a letter.

"Well, my boy," said I, "I've done worse things for me than that was for you; though that was bad enough."

"No, sir; you ain't no bad man," said he.

"Yes, I am; but you and I were born different, though neither of us could help it."

Then he showed me his credentials from the prison, and seemed to think it his chief recommendation that his five years had been shortened ten days for good behavior.

He told me of the "licks," as he called them, with the raw hide, and of the dungeon and starving as punishments.

The United States Government had given him a railroad ticket back to Alabama, and $1.10 in money; for this great and good government of ours delivers a prisoner back where it catches him. Another yellow boy had been sent to his liberty in Texas, the two coming as far as Cincinnati together. The yellow boy had gone on, and left this boy to wait for a later train. This boy was lonesome, and among strangers. He had just parted with his only friend, a boyish companion in guilt, disgrace, and punishment.

"Why did you approach me, and tell me this bad about yourself?" said I.

"I couldn't help tellin' you, sir. I *had* to tell somebody," said he.

Then I did a lot of thinking about as swift as lightning.

Here was a human being; he knew nothing; he had nothing except his crime and the pride of having expiated it, and the recommendation of having shortened the five years ten days by good behavior. He was too innocent to be ashamed of it. His skin was black; but how I wished my soul were as innocent and white as his!

Then for the first time came to me the sweet thought of the beneficence of expiation, — when the punished soul can say: "I have suffered enough: I am innocent again."

Now I had to say to him a hard thing:

"My boy, you have done yourself no harm by telling me all this about yourself; but don't ever in your life tell anybody else. They will think worse of you for it; nearly everybody will. Be a good boy, and let people believe you have always been good."

A cloud came over his face, and he

looked ashamed; but back of it a mute consciousness seemed to say: "What *can* I talk about? I have nothing else."

Here I thought the consolations of religion would ordinarily be offered him; and while he was thanking me for some coins I gave him, the look seemed to come into his face that I certainly must be religious; so I said:

"You may suppose that I am a Christian?"

"Yes," said he.

"I am not," said I.

At our parting he gave me the cold, gripless, tapering hand that belongs to one born without either aggressive or inhibitive powers.

We both said "Goodby," he not knowing, and I forgetting, that "Goodby" meant originally "God be with you."

He was the most frank, honest, and,

at present, most innocent person I have met in many a day.

When and where in the universe will John Gandy and I meet again?

THE HAWK, THE CROW, AND THE HEN.

―――o―――

"Why do you sit so quietly here upon the tree?" said a passing hawk to a crow.

"I am waiting for that hen upon her nest yonder to lay an egg for my breakfast," said the crow.

"Ho! ho!" said the hawk; "before she furnishes you your breakfast, she shall afford me my dinner."

Whereupon, with one swoop he robbed the hen of her life and the crow of his breakfast.

MORAL:

Two acts or intentions may each be bad, and yet one worse than another.

THE PRIEST AND THE SAGE.

———o———

A priest met a sage upon the highway.
"Who art thou?" said the priest.

"How can I tell thee in few words?" replied the sage.

"If thou art not ashamed of thyself and thy calling, thou canst soon tell who thou art," said the priest.

"If I tell thee who men say that I am, or who I think I am, I should be telling thee only two opinions of myself, which might be in error in either case," replied the sage.

"I can ask thy neighbors their opinion of thee, but thou alone canst tell me thy opinion of thyself: speak," said the priest, "or I will belabor thee with my staff."

"I am only a man walking to yonder town to buy some bread for my repast. What more I am I know not," replied the sage.

"Thou art a useless vagabond," said the priest. "I am a priest, and I know the altar where I minister."

The sage started on, murmuring: "Yes, yes; the Chinee knoweth his Joss-House; the Hindoo knoweth his temple; the priest knoweth his altar; the dog knoweth his kennel, and the ass knoweth his crib."

Tranquillity.

———o———

Perhaps the highest development which civilization may be expected to achieve will be to enable the individual to *attain unto tranquillity*. This will mean a state of healthful reciprocation, or harmony with one's environment. The individual will resist the encroachments of environment enough for self-preservation, and use it sufficiently to promote healthy, evenly balanced advancement. Individual nervous systems will not then vary so often and so widely from the sane and tranquil type which illustrates the highest development of man. By that time society will have become so perfectly organized that the individual will know that he cannot injure another without injuring society, and that he cannot injure society without injuring himself. Instead of joy or happiness being restricted to only a few moments, or, at most, only a few hours of a whole human life, it will then include most of the years which intervene between the intended birth and the normal death of the individual. One year then will be worth more than a whole life is worth at present; just as one year of the life of a civilized man is worth more than a whole cycle of the life of a savage. A child born to his natural length of life in that sort of social and individual tranquillity would be heir to more than if born to a thousand years of the present state of civilization.

There are two ideas which are equally inclusive, — *Liberty*, *Justice*. The execution of them in the world, united with wise living, would soon develop both individual and social tranquillity.

The majority of men and women at present do not spend their time thinking how they shall do justice, but how they shall advantage their own selfishness by injustice toward others. They do not study how they themselves and others may be free, but how they may enslave others, and they themselves remain libertines.

Doing justice, makes the doer free ; and receiving justice leaves one free to do. To give liberty makes the giver free. How do you know it does ? Every one knows it who has tried it. None would know what justice is if somebody had not suffered injustice. None would know what liberty is if somebody had not endured bonds.

I don't like to give humanity and civilization up in despair.

ABOUT WOMAN.

―――o―――

I am convinced that women know some things which men do not know. She whose heart-beats have forced her own blood through the heart and veins of another being knows something which men cannot know. Woman's being is interwoven a little closer than man's with the mysteries of birth, life, and death. In all time women have been called superstitious. They have sought oracles and sooth-sayers, and believed in an invisible world, and in subtile, incomprehensible influences. In her instincts and experiences of motherhood, in her lone and silent vigils of the night or of solitude, she has felt that she was a little nearer than man the instrument which fate uses to promote the ends of existence. Men have not heeded this enough; they have overlooked it, brushed it aside, or trampled it down, in their mad rush for the cruder things of life. But I am convinced that when all this subtler insight of woman is listened to and encouraged and collated, it will be the nearest a message from the Divine which has ever yet been received by man. While the world has been listening to the male bird perched upon the topmost branch, it has forgotten the silent mate who has hovered, with her warm, downy breast, the very germs that perpetuate the race.

He who will study and try to understand and collate and publish to the world (publish even to woman herself) this finer insight of woman into the mysteries of existence, will add a new chapter to the wisdom of the ages. Neither men nor women have respected woman's intellectuality enough. She may often be mistaken in regard to herself; she may appear absurd, especially to men; she may be bashful about alluding to her mental states and impressions, because they have always been tabooed by men; she has been caused to repress and conceal rather than to cultivate and express them; but the evidences are that she is breaking through these restraints; that she is discovering herself; and, within the next thirty years, I believe we shall see the virile powers of self-knowing woman added to the active and bettering influences of the world.

When civilization shall have reached its ultimate development; when the records of all influences that contributed to it shall have been made up, — I believe the female human element will form the constituent part of it.

Horses, dogs, domestic and wild animals; fishes, birds, and creeping things; plants, the waters, and the sky, — will all have contributed their share to civilization; and male-man will have contributed his. But the female human element — that first and last, best, tenderest, compassionate element of humanity; the one that has been trampled and disregarded; the one that has answered cruelty with tears only; the one that has been brooding over and protecting the eternal verities as embodied in humanity, — this element will come at last to master all, and be as modest then as it is now.

I never had any hope for civilization until I saw evidences of this.

About Motherhood.

---o---

The pre-Christian Jew-woman desired motherhood, because without it she failed of her probable opportunity to become the mother of a king in the person of the prophesied Christ. And this is one of the harms the preaching of a Christ already come has done; it took away the specific hope and ambition of woman. This hope, which might inspire every virgin without respect to rank, also kept her true to herself and to her people. While in her marriage she lost her opportunity of becoming the actual mother of the Christ, she still retained the hope that she might be one of his progenitors.

It is the hope the gentile women of the world have in motherhood that will most influence the tendencies of civilization. Show me the rewards of motherhood held before the women of a nation, and I will prophesy the ultimate civilization of that nation. What are the rewards of American motherhood? Of the European? Of the Chinese? Of the Hindu? Of the Hottentot? Is the American mother like the hen who knowingly hovers her brood for the market? If, perchance, a child be intentionally begotten in America, what is the hope that inspires the heart of the mother? Is it for the church at the behest of the priest? Is it for love? Is it for the State? Is it for the completion of her own being; for the satisfying of the longing of the mother heart? Is it for the man whom, perchance, she loves, hates, or fears? Is it for pieces of silver? Is it for civilization? Is it for humanity? Is it that she feels herself a part of the eternal economy of the universe; and failing, or degrading this, she would fail being the nearest possible to the Divine? Or, fearing that, living only once, and failing to perpetuate herself in offspring, she would die forever?

Upon the answer American women give depends the hope of our civilization. It may be that a certain reward or hope of motherhood is better suited to one stage of civilization than to another; but whatever its character, let it be the highest of which the woman is capable. Better any reward — any hope — than to be the mother of the unwelcome children of accident or hate. I dare to say that any woman who eschews enforced celibacy, who refuses to sell herself into matrimony or out of it, but who seeks the noblest motherhood possible for her, is worthy of the highest respect.

Alas for the woman who is the mother of nothing!

DO NOT SELL.

Do not sell your preachin'; do not barter the children of your brain, nor the emotions of your heart. Who can bring the best of himself to the marts of men and stand over it for sale as a market-woman does her vegetables? Nobody who ever wrote or sung or carved that which will be immortal, ever rose, shivering in the dim morning light, and trudged it to market.

For monetary gain you may traffic in material things, except your own body and the bodies of others. And severely I charge that you refuse to become rich by withholding from the laborer his just wage. Do not use thy tongue or pen or hand in fear, nor yet in servitude : but in freedom.

Live so, and neither kings, nor station, nor the plaudits of men can add to you ; and you will be worthy the name of man or woman.

Fighting for a Potato-Patch.

An Irishman and an Englishman were engaged in combat, each claiming the exclusive right to the same potato-patch. The Irishman was under, and the Englishman had nearly pounded the life out of him, when the Irishman exclaimed :

"Shtop fightin', my friend ! Be aisy a minit ! By the Holy Vargin ! What fools we are for fightin' over this thing !

You go in partnership with me, and then we can both have it."

"Never!" cried the Englishman, resuming the fight; "for if I go in partnership with you, you will have the potato-patch and me, too. Your race is noted for its appetite for potatoes."

MORALS:

1. Be not too generous, but suspect the proposals of a defeated enemy.
2. The proposal of the Roman Catholics to the Protestants for union.

THE VAIN GARDENER.

A gardener who possessed a good deal of genius, and had exercised much care and skill during a number of years, had succeeded in rearing some fine fruit-trees which stood near the public highway.

The season in which the trees should bear having arrived, the gardener was delighted to find them loaded with fruit of excellent quality. But so proud was he of his skill, and so anxious for the world to know of his success, that he could not wait for the fruit to ripen and the leaves to fall in the autumn. So he secured ladders and picked the green leaves off the trees so that the thick clusters of fruit might appear to the astonished view of the passersby, by which he expected to soon extend his fame.

However, the trees, being robbed of their leaves through which they supported life and nourished their fruit, soon withered; and the fruit dried up and fell to the ground unripe.

"That gardener is a fool," said the passersby.

MORAL:

Authors, artists, and public persons who seek fame prematurely.

THE WIFE OF A WOLF.

A fat, well-grown ewe lamb once fell in love with a wolf; and when he found it out he was much pleased, and married her; for he thought well of enjoying her youthful tenderness for a season, and then making a meal of her. But before he could carry his plans into execution he was taken in some of his depredations and killed by the hunter.

His gentle wife mourned in due form for a year, and then took an honest ram from her own tribe for a second husband.

The ram was well pleased with his bargain until he found that she desired and expected him to behave as the wolf had done.

"Alas!" said the ram, "the enemy of my race has poisoned my cup of happiness, for he has corrupted the manners and tastes of my wife."

MORAL:

It is better to marry the widow of a gentleman than of a rogue.

THE CONSPIRING ANIMALS.

Once upon a time, in a small open field surrounded by deep jungles, the lion, the tiger, the leopard, the hyena, the bear, the wolf, the fox, the boa-constrictor, the hawk, the eagle, and other flesh-eating animals, met in convention to devise means and methods for the better securing their prey. "For," said they, "we flesh-eating and blood-drinking animals are the smartest and noblest of all; we are the true aristocracy. We should be friends instead of enemies. The herbivorous animals are our natural prey; and if we aid one another we may live better and easier." Whereupon they held a great feast united with much merriment. They made so much noise of roaring, howling, and yowling in their revelry, that they attracted the attention of the herbivorous animals of the forest, who secretly sent a committee in the darkness to report what was going on. They appointed on this committee the hare for her acuteness of hearing, the magpie for her loquacity, and the deer for his fleetness of foot.

The hare, with her great ears and eyes, heard and saw much that almost chilled her timid heart with fear; and the magpie and the deer had all they could do to prevent her running away. The magpie almost strangled herself with her chattering loquacity, and the deer stamped his little foot in mock boldness of front.

The carnivorous animals were unconscious of being observed by the committee, and would have laughed in derision if they had known they were.

When the committee returned and made such report as they could, the herbivorous animals resolved to organize an attack upon the assembled revellers.

They placed the elephant, the rhinoceros, the hippopotamus, the horse, and the bull in front; and, following them, came the elk, the camel, the giraffe, the deer, the wild boar, the sheep, and a multitude of other animals, down to the smallest squirrel. Among the whole troop were many jackasses, who tried to direct the march, and made great show of courage from the rear of the column.

There was great carnage, although the carnivora, being glutted with feasting, were not inclined to fight. (It was on this occasion that the ass kicked the dead lion, as related in Æsop's fable.) Many of the herbivora were slain, but the carnivora were finally overpowered by numbers, and few escaped; and to this day they are not numerous in the world, and are compelled to take their prey, not by boldness, but by stealth.

MORALS:

1. When prominent politicians, prelates, corporations, and trusts, who were formerly enemies, become friends, the people should suspect conspiracy.
2. The extravagance and revelry of the wealthy and official classes should alarm the masses of the people.
3. The honest, plain people may finally become aroused and unite to defend their rights, so that they can be taken only by stealth.

JUPITER AND THE BIRDS.

Jupiter once commanded the birds to all fly over a certain large field, and each bring back what it should find.

When the birds returned and had assembled about the god, each brought forward what it had found and laid it at the feet of Jupiter.

The dove had found grains of wheat; the robin had found a berry; the humming-bird brought flowers; the hawk brought a mouse and a young chicken; the nightingale came forward singing, saying she had found a new song inspired by the beauty of the field; the eagle had found a lamb; the vulture had found carrion; the woodpecker had found worms and flies; the stork had found a fish; and the wild-duck had found herbs and grasses.

When all the birds had deposited what they had found, it was a sight such as had never met the eye of bird or god before.

"You see," said Jupiter, "you have

each found what it was his or her nature to look for. Each bird, except the nightingale, has brought before me a prey. Some have been cruel, some filthy, and many of you commonplace. But the nightingale has brought a new song of joy into the world, for which nothing has suffered. Henceforth she shall be the peerless Queen of Song; and, as for the rest of you, your voices, your beaks, and plumage shall forever accord with what you have this day shown your natures to be."

MORALS:

1. In passing through life persons find what they are looking for.
2. Our mode of life modifies our features, our tastes and manners, and our natural powers.

ABOUT MARRIAGE.

The ideal of monogynous and monandrous marriage in the United States, if interfered with as little as possible by the State, and not at all by the Church, is good enough ; in fact, it is a beautiful thing, *if it hits*. But this argues nothing in favor of the institution. Such a very large percentage of marriages do not hit, that the propriety and advantage of the institution at all is being questioned. In any case, where a marriage turns out to be approximately ideal, it is not to be set to the praise or blame of the institution. Such cases are instances of successful sex-selection or sex-mating. Marriage or no marriage would not make such a couple live together with greater satisfaction and fidelity to each other.

The institution of marriage is all right in itself to meet the objects of its origin, viz., to protect the relation and offspring and property rights of a perfectly sex-mated couple; but, too often, the form is mistaken for the substance or principle of the relation. Normal sex-selection is interfered with in the majority of cases, and for the incompatible results the institution of marriage is blamed.

Of all evils which militate against the welfare and development of society, it is probable that the conventional interference with normal sex-selection is the greatest. It causes many children to be born of hate, and deprives the parties to the relation of that benign influence which would otherwise be received from associating with a normal mate.

The so-called lower animals choose their mates with unerring success; and the uniformity and perfection of their reproduction is one of the wonderful and beautiful things in nature. In this regard man is the exceptional fool of the world; and the outrages which he inflicts upon nature avenge themselves wofully upon his offspring. It is highly probable that there is hardly an imperfection of mind or body that is not, in a great measure, traceable to this defect of human society; and it is equally probable that if conventional interference with the mating of human beings were entirely abated, man would soon develop the power of mating as successfully as the lower animals do. So rarely does perfect sex-mating occur in civilized society that normal sex-propensities are hardly known, and are certainly not understood.

The true marriage occurs in the hearts of the lovers,—in their known congeniality of mind and body; and what is ordinarily called the marriage is only the announcement to the world that the true marriage has previously occurred.

Civilized man and woman is so sensitive to what (for want of a better name) may be called personal magnetism, or the agreeableness or disagreeableness of physical proximity or touch, that congeniality in this respect must be regarded as an essential in successful mating. So many people have been born of mismated parents,—so many people are perverts in a greater or less degree,—that perfectly mated normal relations are exceedingly uncommon in civilized society. Many persons do live together as man and wife, with apparent and, as they themselves believe, with great happiness; but it is probable that not over one in one hundred of such couples realize the highest possible felicity of such relations.

It is romantically and universally believed in the world that for every person there is, somewhere in the wide world, one perfectly ideal mate; and the belief is probably founded in fact. It forms the basis of romance, especially for the young; and those who find, or believe they find, their own and only world-wide mates are the blessed among mankind. All else in the world is as dross as compared with this.

Whether people often, or ever do, find this one only world-wide mate cannot be known, for there are many millions of possible mates in the world; but true it is, and of frequent experience, that some persons are better suited to each other than others are. And though two persons may marry who are not world-wide mates, yet they may be so approximately mated that they go through life with tolerable contentment. How each person is to find his or her world-wide or approximate mate, and how they may know, of a certain, before public marriage, that they have so found them, are the two most vital questions to every young person, and to the whole of human society.

This essay is already too long, but the author believes that by his study of the mating instincts and habits of the lower animals, and by a practical study of the actual instincts and the actual normal courtship experiences of well-mated humans, he may point out some reliable guides to persons who are seeking the best mates possible for them in the world. How to find, and know that you have found, your mate, is the question. The author must leave this question for a future publication.

No person should feel damaged by breach of promise to marry; but rather account himself fortunate in discovering before, instead of after marriage, that he or she was not wanted. The courts should so hold.

No couple should marry or remain married who need the restraints of law or custom to hold them together; for the natural evils of remaining together are greater than the conventional harms of breaking asunder. Wedlock should not be a bond (no bond can be a "holy bond"), but a relation gladly entered into from the freest choice, and joyfully continued without distraint or obligation.

Painting, Sculpture, Poetry, and the

Drama have been the great critics of all the ages; and their sublimest creations—embracing the very *motif* and object of their existence—have encircled and upheld that one eternal principle, that sex-selection should be left absolutely free, untrammelled by family, or feud, or property, or rank, or race. The best of the world believe in love. There have been wars and duels and sacrifices for it. The whole world believes in the unerring choice of love; but who can look back, over much or little experience, and say he or she is certain of love? That is our question in another form.

When married people find they have been mistaken it is criminally sinful to have children. Every child has a right to be born of parents who love each other. The sooner a mismated couple cease their relations the better. Take care that the marriages are made right, and the divorces will take care of themselves; there will be none.

JUPITER AND THE ANTS.

A colony of ants had built the highest mound they could, and were dwelling in it with commendable satisfaction, until some of them discovered that the houses of a city near by were not natural objects, but that they were the dwellings of a larger sort of animal called man.

At this they became dissatisfied with their own lot, and complained to Jupiter for having made an animal so much larger than themselves, and who built mounds of so much greater magnificence than theirs.

"Looked upon with the eye of a god," replied Jupiter, "there is not much difference between you."

MORAL:

The greatest are not worthy of envy.

THE HEIFER AND THE ROSES.

A young heifer, who, for the most part, was like the other heifers of the herd, had the opinion that she, herself, was very refined; and that grass, as a food, was too ordinary for her. She said grass gave color and beauty to the landscape, but, as for food, it was plebeian. So she went about smelling roses and other flowers, and never eating anything.

She grew very thin; for she kept going about everywhere, always smelling roses, and eating nothing. And everywhere she went she kept m-o-o-ing and complaining to the other cattle that she was starving.

Some of the other heifers, and even a few of the bull-calves, sympathized with her; but at last she came to an old bull, to whom she complained, who said:

"Alas! madam, you will have to eat grass like the rest of us."

MORAL:

The destitute æsthete or sentimentalist.

The Ox with the Silver Flanks.

A Dream.

It was summer-time. I had been drooning over books and the deeper problems of human life. I became drowsy, and threw myself across my bed. I lay upon my side, with my knees drawn up and my hands under my chin, as babes do in their mothers' womb.

And I slept and dreamed.

I was in a strange place, as if it were the ruins of an Acropolis. And there were columns and arches and halls and colonnades and fallen and broken capitals. I stood with one whom I knew not and who spake not.

And off to the right I could not see, but I knew that men were torturing and slaughtering many cattle. And presently I saw one great dark-gray ox with a mad plunge and struggle, break out into a field away from the slaughterers. Of such fierce, frantic, wild beauty I had never seen an animal before. His long, graceful horns were like polished alabaster tipped with ebony. His eyes, nostrils, and hoofs were black as jet, and surrounded with silver. His flanks were like arches of light.

Across the great field he galloped away, not caring for fences, ditches or furrows. Men gathered in pursuit from every direction. Some were on horseback with lassoes and spears, and others ran on foot with javelins and ropes and thongs. They entangled him in ropes and chains, and attached to them sleds and logs and horses and men. Still he plunged on, never attacking his tormentors, never resisting except by flight. How I wished he might go free! How I wished he knew I wished him to be free!

Presently he tore himself loose from the thongs, and, outstripping all, came plunging through the ruins where we stood. He, whom I knew not and who spake not, hid behind a wall. I stood in an arch through which the ox, who was almost upon me, must surely pass. Too late for flight, I leaped and caught the keystone of the arch, and, drawing myself up, hung suspended until the frantic animal should gallop through beneath me. To my consternation, he stopped suddenly beneath me, and his great white horns were touching my body. When I could cling no longer, I let myself down upon his horns, which changed to be the gentle arms of a great, beautiful woman. She placed me standing upon the ground, and I was not afraid of her, but I was as much afraid of her pursuers as she was. And I remembered I had wished the ox to be free.

"I cannot endure their pursuit many days longer; how shall I escape?" she said to me with a calm, unresentful, and infinitely patient voice. I thought she felt she might be wronging her pursuers if she escaped from them immediately.

With this I began to climb down a steep precipice, which, I regretted, she, as ox or woman, would hesitate to attempt; and I said to her, or to the ox (I cannot remember which):

"Down through this deep valley, and over that sunlit hill yonder, they cannot follow."

Then I awoke and heard the chimes of evening church-bells, and I knew that women were still praying and suffering just as they had done for thousands of years.

In a Certain Country.

In a certain country there were five table-lands or plains between the shore of the sea and the summit of the mountains. The plain nearest the sea was the lowest, and each successive plain was higher than the preceding one.

And it so happened that the Government of that country decreed that if certain of the inhabitants of the lowest plain struggled hard and contended with one another (often to the wounding and destruction of many), the survivors should be promoted to the next higher plain. Here the operations of struggle and contention were repeated with even greater fierceness and cruelty; and the survivors were elevated to the next plain above. Thus they continued until they had reached the highest plain of all, near the summit of the mountains.

As most of the inhabitants were born on the lowest plain, and as the numbers of the higher plains, even to the highest, were constantly replenished from below, the population of the several plains remained about equal; and the competitive contention was equally keen upon them all,—even to the highest; for here the inhabitants were in mortal fear of being thrown down again. Indeed it was the fate of some, after having gained the highest, and their powers began to fail, to be thrown successively back to the lowest plain again.

But one who had gained the highest plain, and who was wiser than all the rest, complained to the Government, saying:

"I have been deceived. Here I find competition and struggle more severe and cruel than ever; and men die with a look of contention and selfishness upon their faces. I will return to the peaceful place of my birth, and listen, and wait, and rest by the shore of the sea."

And going down, he told all who were struggling up; but they hearkened not, and are still continuing unto this day.

THE AUTHOR AND THE READER.

The author of this book is not a doctor, that he wants the reader for a patient; nor a lawyer, that he wants the reader for a client; nor a preacher, that he wants the reader for a pew-filler; nor a merchant, that he wants the reader for a customer; nor a teacher, that he wants the reader's children for pupils; nor a university professor, that he fears the influence that appointed him; nor a politician, that he wants the reader's vote or a place by appointment; nor a laborer, that he wants the reader to employ him; nor a banker, that he wants the reader for a depositor; nor an editor, that he wants the reader's subscription; nor a mendicant, that he wants the reader's aid; nor is he in trouble, that he wants the reader's sympathy; nor is he rich, that he needs the law's protection from the reader's envy; nor is he a professional charity promoter, that he wants the reader's contribution; nor does he desire fame or power. Nor does the author want to sell this book to the reader for gain. Nor is the author a rascal, that he wants the reader for his victim; at least, if he really, at heart, is a rascal, he begs the reader to credit him with having removed himself, as far as possible, from all inducement to practise his rascality.

Now, therefore, since the author has refused to be any of all the foregoing sorts of persons, in order that he might be free ; and since the reader may belong to one or more of the above-mentioned classes, the author begs the reader to remember this when he essays to pass judgment on anything in this book. And if, perchance, the reader hears another inveighing against this book, or against the author, will the reader be pleased to ask such person if he is as free as the author is ? The reader may blame the author for being a fool, or for having published the book at all, but not for insincerity.

If the author shall have made the reader wiser, better, truer, he will be glad ; and if he has hurt the reader's feelings, the reader is to blame for having read the book at all.

A parson, going to church, walked a half-mile out of his way to catch some boys fishing on Sunday; and, having caught them, said :

"Boys, don't you know it hurts my feelings to see you fishing on the Sabbath ?"

The boys replied :

"We are sorry, sir; but you walked a half-mile out of your way to get your feelings hurt."

Having delivered himself of the foregoing prefaces and apologies, the author does not fear even that most terrible of all ogres, the Reading Public.

The Trees and the Gardeners.

A gentleman once employed a number of gardeners to look after his trees. As there were more gardeners than there was work to do, each gardener felt that not only his fame but the permanence of his situation depended upon the showing he could make upon those trees, when the gentleman should return at the end of the season.

Each gardener wanted to select the most central and public trees to exploit his work upon.

For this reason they strove with one another and disputed among themselves as to the treatment each tree needed. One would contend that a tree leaned too much this way, and he would bend it in the opposite direction ; another declared it leaned too much that way, and again strained it in a different direction. One contended that some of its branches were too low, and lopped them off. Another declared the tree was too high for its width, and he cut the top off. Another asserted the trunk and limbs were too slender to sustain the great weight of leaves, flowers, and fruit he intended it should bear, and he slit the bark up to give them room to enlarge. Another punctured the trunk in many places in order to make the wood gnarly, so that in fifty years it would make beautiful sounding-boards for fiddles, averring that the music of future ages depended upon it. Another lopped off the side branches, saying they were so long they would shade the roots. Another would cut off all the original branches and graft on other kinds, so that the same tree might bear a variety of fruit. One carted loads of manure to the roots, and another carted it away, saying it was not the right kind, or that it was too much or not enough. One said it should be watered with a mixture of chemicals, and another that it should be kept dry. One insisted that half the blossoms should be plucked off, so that the others should come to better maturity. Some thought it should be forced to bear and mature earlier, to avoid the frosts of the season, and others that it should be retarded.

When the gentleman returned he found his once beautiful orchard in a sad plight indeed. "Alas!" said he, "the number and officiousness of my gardeners have spoiled my trees;" and, taking the gardeners to an obscure part of his grounds, he pointed out to them a tree they had overlooked, which was laden with fruit and was well grown and symmetrical, except one or two branches which, by their irregularity, gave graceful prominence to the general beauty of the tree.

"This tree," said he, "has flourished by your neglect. If you had only put food and light and air and moisture within reach of the trees and then *let them alone*, my beautiful orchard had not been despoiled and barren."

MORALS:

1. The competition and officiousness of so-called educators is a harm.

2. The child should be put among proper environment and then—*let it alone*.

3. The world is education-mad, both ecclesiastical and secular.

4. Such characters as Abraham Lincoln and Jesus, by the obscurity of their situations, escaped the influence of the schools.

About the Fable.

The words *fable*, fame, fate, infant, phase, phantom, phenomenon, are of similar etymological origin. In the ultimate idea of its etymology the word *fable* means: not speaking, yet making to shine, to appear, to make plain, to make known. And this is just what the true fable does; it does not speak or mention the truth or moral, but makes it appear with great boldness through describing an entirely different set of circumstances.

Of all sorts of writing, successful fabling is the rarest. There have been fewer successful fablers than of any other sort of writer. Only two or three fablers have made themselves remembered by the world; and yet neither the allegory, the parable, the simile, the metaphor, nor any other sort of illustrative form of speech, can equal the fable in the universality of its appreciation by the human race.

By the utter and evident disregard of probability in the statement of its narrative, the fable throws into bold relief— makes unmistakably clear and plain— the inmost traits of human character and the rightest rules of human conduct.

Every poem is, in some sense, a fable, and the best of fables are, in a certain sense, poetical. The fable need not, necessarily, be humorous; but it must be witty. It pleases mainly by the directness and simplicity of its style; by being utterly impersonal; by making the reader believe he advises himself, and by reserving the point of the story to burst upon the surprise of the reader at the last.

The disposition to fable seems to be natural to the human mind. The greatest of men have delighted in fable. Even children have an inclination to exaggerate and enfable their every-day plays and experiences into the uncommon and unknown.

While some myths have seemed to obtain quite universally, they disappear with the advancement of science and the improvement of reason; indeed the myth is the product of faith and unreason;

while the fable accompanies the age of paramount enlightenment, and illustrates the deepest possible insight into human motive and character. The fable will accompany civilization and literature to their highest development. The best of fables will doubtless live forever. They will live when their authors shall have been forgotten amid the myths of the past.

If the author of this book shall have produced even one successful fable, he shall feel that his thought will long survive to influence his fellow-man.

THE NEWSPAPER—THE THEATRE.

The greatest civilizing influences of the world are the Newspaper and the

Theatre. At present the newspaper influence is the greater of the two; but in time the theatre influence will overshadow all. The author cannot take space now to explain why this is true. These two greatest of all agencies have had the same hand-maiden, viz., Applied Mechanics. They have also had one and the same enemy, viz., the Church. From this heretofore implacable foe they have, as yet, one danger: having failed in her efforts to prevent or destroy them, she will now attempt to claim them as her children, and pervert and control them for her use.

It will be noticed that these two greatest civilizing agencies are immaterial. Their greatest manifestations of art and power come and go as peaceful, as transitory, as evanescent as the night. They may surpass the very genii of the myths in their brilliant and wonder-working productions; but when the curtain falls, or the day is done, they are no more. A new day, a new night, brings a new expenditure of genius; two productions are never alike. They follow one another like the waves that expend themselves against the shore, dissolving back into the unresting ocean; but they are never alike.

Art is great, but she has always sold herself to the powers that be; she has never fought ahead of her time and built bridges for humanity to pass. Wherever she has been free she has been noble and ennobling.

I wish these three—Art, the Newspaper, the Theatre—to have freedom; and then I shall not despair of civilization.

Two Letters to Elza.

[There are about seventy of the "Letters to Elza" in existence, touching many social subjects. Paul Pinhook is the author's *nom de plume* to his humorous and sentimental writings.]

My dear Elza:

I'm tired of poor people. I was once poor myself, the time you can remember well; but I'm tired of them now, anyhow. They are disagreeable.

Imagine, if you can, a horse like, in most respects, the average civilized horse, in the midst of a clover-field up to his knees and up to his eyes in clover. He is sleek and happy in his horse-way: or rather would be happy were it not that a multitude of poor devils of horses crowd around his field, starved, bony, hollow-eyed; or if allowed to cross his pasture they are muzzled and dare not eat; some of them hoof-sore and dying. Every sweet clover-blossom our sleek horse plucks with his white teeth and firm nibbling lip is coveted, is longed for, by the perishing lookers on; and he is conscious of it.

And yet, he dares not throw down his fence nor unmuzzle them; there would not be one clover blossom left—aye, even the very roots would be plucked out, and he become destitute, starved as they. I am that sleek horse. I am unhappy.

Ah, thou meek and gentle Jew, who didst take neither scrip nor staves, but didst pluck thy repast from the berries of the field: thou hast taught me this impractical sympathy for the starving, the distressed and the forlorn ; and I am unhappy.

———

Yes, Elza, with your gentle heart, when I say " I am tired of the poor," you will understand. I was born poor, I was reared poor; every hard and burdened path of theirs I have trodden. When my feet were bleeding and my eyes were dust-blinded and tearful, did some one pity me then? If so, I knew it not. I wish I knew where he or she is to-day ; I would go and stand by the side of that heart of pity and say : " Thou art like Jesus ; I love thee."

But I am tired of the poor. My sympathy is worn out, and, I fear, is becoming calloused.

Knowledge of the poor leaves you to despair or to become calloused. Dare I wish I had not this knowledge? Dare I wish I had been born rich and therefore without experience, without knowledge?

I could have had fine theories then; but what a different heart! None but the soldier knows what it is to be wounded and left to the darkness, the unceasing rain, the unpitying night and sky of the battle-field. Only the poor know what it is to be poor. Only those who have been poor can have and know the heart of the poor.

A canopy arches the way from the massive steps of a mansion down to the curbstone. Closed carriages with their trappings come and go in turn. It is night. Halting aside upon the pavement are a man and a woman; a small shawl over her head, the Easter bonnet of the poor. A basket is on his left arm and she snuggles close to his other elbow, and over them he holds a cotton umbrella; for it is drizzling and a keen wind is blowing.

They are looking toward the plate glass window ablaze with light. The very cost of the glass would be a fortune to them.

They start to go away, but music, such as only comes from the homes of the rich, speeds out upon the unpurchased air. They hesitate, linger, because they love music. It ceases; they say something low and gentle to each other, and move on into the darkness.

Within are flying feet, encased in slippers so delicate and white, the woman on the street would rub her hand twice upon her apron before touching them, lest she might soil them; and stockings, and laces and lingerie and flounces and the very gossamer threads spun by the worm;

and corsage and flowers, and jewels, and flossy and fluffy hair, and brilliant eyes, and wines and ices and banks of flowers, and chandeliers jewelled with lights.

Elza, I have been on both sides of that glittering barrier of glass. What was I on one side; what on the other?

Such as I was outside, such as I was inside that pane of glass, and such as I am now, I am

Your unwavering,

PAUL PINHOOK.

MY DEAR ELZA:

I was outside of the glittering barrier of glass that night. I was outside in a double sense, for I had not yet gotten my elegant lodgings; and, as I have before told you, I was therefore not considered a person of sufficient consequence to be recognized and invited by people of consequence.

And I am glad I was outside that night—outside in the rain and the darkness. My heart is different now from what it would have been if I had been inside. That hour outside was worth many a year inside. I heard and understood what that man and woman said to each other as they "moved on into the darkness."

"I'm glad they have some pleasures. I wish we could know they love each other as we do," said the man.

"I wish they had a sweet little home like ours," said the woman.

Like the wandering, homeless wight I was, I followed them; for what I heard them say was like a mist of light that enhaloed them; and it led me on.

Imagine yourself, if you can, following

two such hearts, two such lovers—amid the rain and the bewildering dismal shadows of the night.

' I sometimes do queer things—led by the impulse of my heart—such things as a woman might do had she the freedom of a man. I walked past the cottage I saw them enter. I hesitated, stood on tip-toe, and looked through the bright window-panes into the cozy room glowing with the light of an open fire and a lamp that stood upon a table. I saw a strong man with tranquil countenance and hands able and willing to labor. I saw the hale, capable, cheerful housewife in an adjoining room preparing the evening meal, and the rosy children about them. I felt guilty of almost desecrating their unconscious happiness by looking upon it. Here was the poet's "Cotter's Saturday Night."

I walked away in the rain and the darkness. I thought of love, and of God; and then of splendid poverty. I felt alone and dismal as the night; I had gotten an ideal; I had found human contentment. I was lonesome, I say, but I felt that somehow, somewhere, sometime, I, too, should find contentment and happiness.

I was a long way from home—from that ideal, I mean. I was years away from it—how many I could not tell. I had never had a home since I rocked the cradle for my mother or picked up chips for her in the old wood-pile on the farm. That is only a memory now, but it came back to my heart that night like a sigh from one who has been weeping. I was tired-hearted that night as I turned my coat-collar up and leaned toward the rain that came swishing into my face as I walked solitary toward my desolate lodgings. I went up one, two, three flights of stairs, and back through the long narrow hall. Only ashes were in my grate, and only ashes were in my heart. The lamp was dim and the air damp. In one short hour I had seen splendid poverty and honest contentment, and I myself was an example of intelligent misery. I was miserable, and I knew it; I could see it; I could feel it; I could almost hear it in the mocking silence of the damp dead air—but I did not despair. I could have only vaguely told you why, but I went to sleep that night with almost impatience for the morning's dawn to begin anew the journey of my life; for I had found the silencer of despair and the leaven of hope in the beautiful ideal of the Cottagers' Home.

The next day I wrote you one of my old cheerful letters—perhaps a shade more tender—and signed myself as I do now,
    Your devoted,
      Paul Pinhook.

Tell Me.

Tell me who opens his mouth to speak except for pay of gold; or who lifts his hands and bows his head except that laurels may be placed upon his brow: tell me, and I will hearken unto him.

I'M TIRED.

I'm tired of preachers and teachers and book-writers. I wish they'd shut up and let me alone. I wish they'd let the great, tired-hearted common people alone. We are tired of being brayed at, and barked at, and cawed at, and hissed at. Let us alone. Wait until we ask you to save us, and educate us, and civilize us. Perhaps when we think on't a little, we won't prefer your way. Go away and let us alone. We're tired now.

THE END.

www.ingramcontent.com/pod-product-compliance
Lightning Source LLC
Chambersburg PA
CBHW020758230426
43666CB00007B/744